TOTALLY FRANK

This book is dedicated to my late granny Hannah, my mum and late dad, and my four children, who have all helped me through life. My love for them is unconditional.

TOTALLY FRANK

THE FRANK McGARVEY STORY

Frank McGarvey
with Ronnie Esplin

MAINSTREAM
PUBLISHING

EDINBURGH AND LONDON

First published in Great Britain in 2008 by
MAINSTREAM PUBLISHING COMPANY
(EDINBURGH) LTD
7 Albany Street
Edinburgh EH1 3UG

ISBN 9781845963644

A catalogue record for this book is available
from the British Library

Typeset in Caslon and Century Gothic

Printed in Great Britain by
Clays Ltd, St Ives plc

ACKNOWLEDGEMENTS

I must be the only person in the world to write a book and not want it published. The day it hits the shops, I hope I'm out of the country, somewhere such as Hawaii would be nice, but that's unlikely. I will probably be in and around Glasgow, where I have been for most of the 52 years I've had to revisit in the course of writing this book. The journey has not been an easy one to make. I've gone back to places that I didn't really want to go again, and I've had to reveal things that I don't really want people to know. I've found that the depths of your soul can be a dark place. This book might help me, I don't know, but if it helps just one family to understand and cope with the problems that gambling can cause, it will have been worth it.

There are many people to thank, none more so than all those at Gamblers Anonymous who have supported me over the years. Their efforts have helped thousands of people in Scotland to stop gambling.

From the world of professional football, Alex and Martin Ferguson, Alex Miller, Ricky Macfarlane, Billy McNeill and John Clark deserve my gratitude.

Thanks to George Pratt, who had the original book idea and who provided crucial information and statistics. George and his wife Evelyn have been great to me over the years. St Mirren fan and historian Jim Crawford, Liverpool historian Eric Doig, Paul Walker, Dave Ball, Brian Johnson, Alan Henderson, Matt McGlone, Paul McGurk and Linda McHugh provided invaluable input and help.

I would also like to thank Jackie, Joe Boyce, Kenny Lang, Ian Wilson, Walter Horne, Alan Minster, Ian French, Tom Smith, Brian Murphy, Bill Shedden, Paul McNulty, Pat and Gerard Mulcahy, Archie and Ann Marie Stormonth, Jimmy and Anne Critchley, and Bill Toy.

Tony Adams's autobiography was an inspiration, and thanks to Alan Brazil for having the courage to speak out against child abuse. That gave me the courage to delve back into a frightening time in my life.

Bill Campbell, Graeme Blaikie, Paul Murphy and Kate McLelland at Mainstream showed professionalism and patience.

I would like to thank the fans of all the clubs I played for, especially the St Mirren supporters who spurred me on at the beginning of my career and the Celtic fans who continue to give me their support. I would also like to sincerely thank the thousands of Rangers fans who have shown me respect by coming up to me and shaking my hand over the years. That means a lot to an ex-Celtic player.

Finally, I would like to thank my children just for being my children.

Frank McGarvey
August 2008

CONTENTS

FOREWORD

Frank first came to my attention when he was making his way in the game at St Mirren. I thought he would be a big success when he moved to Liverpool, but unfortunately it didn't work out for him. You always wonder how a new recruit will turn out, but I thought he would be a steal for any club when I paid a record fee to bring him to Celtic in 1980.

Frank turned out to be a superb signing. He had all the qualities needed for a striker: he was enthusiastic, hard-working, effective in front of goal and someone who could also link the play up. He was also great in the dressing-room, where he would always say or do something daft to entertain the rest of the lads. He was different class in that respect, and it was great to have him around.

What I remember most from his time at Celtic was the day he scored the second goal of a hat-trick against St Mirren at Parkhead. There were about 30 seconds left of the first half when he picked the ball up in the middle of the park, beat a few players and scored a magnificent goal that earned him a tremendous ovation from the Celtic supporters, the likes of which I hadn't heard too often. But he was so overwhelmed by the reception he got from the fans as he walked off that he was in the toilet at half-time being sick as I was trying to talk to the rest of the players.

Unfortunately, you don't see many of Frank's type any more – players who like to take other players on. Defenders would worry when he had the ball, and although he certainly wasn't built like a heavyweight boxer he was fearless on the pitch. No defender could frighten him.

Charlie Nicholas and George McCluskey were different types of players from Frank, and he was a perfect foil for both of them. They knew when to leave Frank alone and when to give him a hand.

I got to know about his gambling problem, but he didn't bring it into the dressing-room, and it certainly didn't affect his performances for Celtic in any way, which is a credit to him.

I became very fond of Frank, and any time I meet him he tells me how it is. He is as honest as the day is long. It's great that he seems to be able to control his gambling these days, and I wish him all the best for the future.

Billy McNeill MBE
August 2008

PROLOGUE

In the summer of 1964, the McGarvey family went to Leven on the east coast of Scotland for our annual holiday. My dad, Edward, gave each of his sons – Andrew, Edward, Joseph and me – a £1 note. It was to last us for the entire week that we were there. I was eight years old, the youngest of the four, and £1 was a lot of money to me.

I wandered into an amusement arcade and changed it into 240 pennies. Within an hour, I had put every one of them into the one-armed bandits. It was my first experience of gambling. I don't know why I did it. I still don't to this day. I had never seen a fruit machine before, so maybe that was the reason. Who knows? But whatever prompted my actions, for the rest of the week, while my brothers were going on the rides at the funfair and eating ice creams and sweets, I was left out.

My dad noticed this and asked me what had happened to my money. I told him that I was keeping it to put it in the bank when I got home. He was taken aback by my apparent sense of responsibility. It was the first time I remember telling a lie, and it was because I had lost money gambling. It was just the beginning. Since then, a small, unquenchable gambling flame has been alight inside me. At times, it has been little more than a pilot light. However, too often it has been an inferno, and during those periods it has had a profoundly negative effect on every part of my life. I am still fighting to keep it under control. Every day.

1

I BELONG TO GLASGOW

In February 2007, I sat at the top table at my benefit dinner in a Glasgow hotel with my four children, Paul, Sean, Scott and Jennifer, and my mother, Mary, and surveyed the 400 or so people who had turned up to honour me, years after my football career had finished. Ian French, who had been my coach at youth level and who had shown endless faith in me as I'd tried to make the grade, was also beside me. He deserved no less for his part in shaping my career. Without him, I would never have become a professional footballer.

I had been piped into the hall, where former Celtic manager Billy McNeill and ex-Parkhead teammates Davie Provan, Roy Aitken and Danny McGrain, my old St Mirren coach Ricky Macfarlane and my friend and ex-Buddies captain Tony Fitzpatrick, guys with whom I had shared some of my most memorable football days, sat in attendance.

I was glad to see that Tom Smith, a friend who had suffered

financially at my hands when I was at my lowest ebb and had almost been beaten by the gambling addiction that has blighted my life, had turned up. Jimmy Wilson, who had taken it upon himself to organise the night, knowing that I could do with a hand at that time, caught my eye, and I hoped he could see how grateful I was. I had lost a bit of self-respect by the time he had come into my life. My post-football life had been difficult, to say the least. I had been divorced from my wife Pauline, estranged from my kids for a long spell and I had lost all the money I had accumulated during a playing career that had taken me from Kilsyth Rangers to St Mirren, Liverpool, Celtic and back to Love Street before spells at Queen of the South, Clyde and Shotts Bon Accord.

I had been worried that, with all my highly publicised problems, nobody would turn up for my big night, but the place was packed, and I couldn't believe the reception I received. It was very humbling, and it took all my willpower to stop myself from crying. Seldom had I found a calm middle ground in a life that had oscillated between the highest highs and the lowest lows. I was just glad to have survived a roller-coaster journey that began in Glasgow on 17 March 1956.

When I made my debut at the Rottenrow Hospital, my parents didn't have a name for me. Being St Patrick's day, you might have expected them to call me Patrick. But it was difficult for people with Catholic names to get jobs in the west of Scotland at that time – so they called me Francis Peter. Their little joke was typical of Glasgow humour, especially in relation to the religious problems that have bedevilled the city for decades. I would get to know all about them soon enough.

My very earliest recollections, however, are all very innocent. We lived in an old tenement building in Dundas Street, across from Queen Street Station in the heart of Glasgow, until I was two years old, and then we moved to a brand-new house at 4 Dungeonhill Road, Easterhouse, in the north-east of the city.

Easterhouse, Castlemilk and Drumchapel were three massive housing schemes built on the north-east, south and west of Glasgow respectively to take the mostly working-class people from the slum areas such as the Gorbals and Dalmarnock. It was a huge movement of people over a relatively short time span, but it was an exciting period for the many families who wanted to escape from the squalor so widely associated with the city.

The first memory I have, although obviously hazy, is being in a furniture van with my dad travelling from Dundas Street to our new abode about five miles from Celtic Park. Our new home, up a 'close' containing five other houses, was much bigger than our previous place, with three bedrooms, a living room, a kitchen and, best of all, an inside toilet and bathroom. Central heating and double glazing, things we take for granted these days, were some time away yet. The coal fire in the living room was the main source of heat. The coal lorry would come around every week, and the coalmen, unrecognisably dark, mysterious figures, would haul the sacks up into the coalbunkers, which were located on the close landings. In winter, when the rest of the house was frozen, you shivered for the first few minutes when you went to bed. But it was still a vast improvement on our previous house, and my mum and dad were well chuffed.

The fundamental problem with those sprawling schemes was that they consisted of houses and little else. Easterhouse's population numbered nearly 60,000 at the end of the 1950s, but a lack of foresight meant that there were few shops and little if any amenities for adults or children. That lack of provision was one reason, albeit not the only one, why those social-housing experiments in some ways failed.

Glasgow's new urban deserts quickly acquired a fearsome reputation for deprivation and violence, which they have struggled to shake off. Many sons and daughters of these places have conveniently left their early days off their CVs after moving elsewhere in Glasgow or out of the city altogether, but not me. I am proud to have been brought up in Easterhouse, and I don't feel stigmatised by it.

The McGarvey boys were just ordinary Glaswegians, all encouraged by our parents to do as well as we could in life. Andrew went on to become a schoolteacher then a lecturer, Edward became a heating engineer and Joseph ended up on the oil rigs after serving his time as an electrician. Of course, with four boys in the house, there were always plenty of fights, and as the youngest I bore the brunt of them. I was also the last to get the hand-me-down clothes, toys and bikes, but I had no complaints. After all, I didn't know any better, and I look back on my childhood and adolescent years with fondness.

My dad, a short man with glasses, was a tough, stubborn Glaswegian but basically a nice wee guy. He was a brilliant electrician, one of the old-style tradesmen who did a job right, no matter how long it took. He worked for various companies, but in his latter years was employed by the lighting department of Glasgow City Council. He never told anyone that he was Frank McGarvey's dad. He and a few of his colleagues used the same barbers at Glasgow Cross, and someone told the barber that Frank McGarvey's dad got his hair cut in his shop. The next time my dad went in, he was chatting away with the barber, who said to him, 'I heard Frank McGarvey's dad comes in here.' My dad just said, 'Is that right?' and moved the conversation on. He was not interested in the limelight or any reflected glory.

My sister Marie arrived after we had settled in to Dungeonhill Road, when I was about ten. Mum and Dad now had five kids to bring up, which required money. This meant lots of overtime for my father. Despite him working long hours and always being tired when he came home, we had a good relationship. He was a very practical person, and he would fix my bike and things like that, which was certainly appreciated. By the time I had a bike passed down to me by my three brothers, it needed plenty of attention.

When my dad was off at weekends, I was always out playing football. Consequently, I spent a lot more time with my mother when I was growing up and was closer to her. Like most mothers of her generation, my mum stayed at home to look after the children. She kept the house spotless, and we were always well fed, not like some of my friends, I'm sad to say. She always seemed to be in the kitchen, and huge pots of soup were her speciality. When I came home from school at lunchtime, I would get a big plate of soup, which was a meal in itself, lots of bread and a plate of custard for dessert. I thought everyone ate like that. But one time I had to go to my pal's house, and his mum gave me a little plate of soup with no bread and then said to us, 'OK, boys, away back to school.' I was starving all afternoon, and it was then that I appreciated my mum's generosity.

We were acutely aware that our parents were doing their best to provide what luxuries they could for the house and their family on a much wider level than soup portions. The only time they went out together, more or less, was to visit my gran in Colston, and neither of them touched alcohol. However, like many working men, my dad faithfully wrote out his Littlewoods coupon on a Friday night, although he never considered that to be gambling. Glasgow has always been associated with heavy drinking, and when I was growing up it was mostly a male problem. You would never see a woman in a pub alone, and there was a sense of shame for a female if she was seen to be drunk. The man in the flat above us was a heavy drinker, which meant most of his wages were squandered down the pub or in the off-licence. His wife would often come down to our house, and she would always comment on the nice furniture we had. Even at a young age, I could sense that she resented her husband for not being able to have the same.

I remember my mum being pleased that we were the first in our close to have a telephone installed. That was a huge thing at the time, and all the neighbours would ask to use it, saving themselves a walk to the public phone box. Owning a car was another significant sign of social one-upmanship. When you could afford to own a car in Easterhouse, that was you made. I was so thrilled when my dad came home with his 1956 Standard Ten, which he had bought for about £100, a veritable fortune in those days.

Holidays were an important part of life for the McGarvey family, and my parents would always take us away in the summer, although places such as Spain and Portugal were still only for reading about in books. I'm not sure if my mum and dad even had passports. Places such as Leven, Rothesay and Burntisland seemed to be on the other side of the world to us anyway, and there was always much excitement boarding the specially commissioned trains at Easterhouse Station that would take us direct to our destinations. A beautiful old steam train was used on the Saltcoats line, which was a big thrill for me and all the other young guys who pretended to be Casey Jones for the day.

Although Easterhouse was united by its working-class population, it was divided by its different churches. The Catholic and Protestant rift always puzzled me. I just couldn't understand why the two factions didn't like each other – after all, we were all Glaswegians. It has never been an issue to me, and I put that down to the way I was raised. I believe bigotry stems from the home, and I wasn't brought up with hate in my heart. I have to thank my mum and dad for that.

As far as I'm concerned, a religious upbringing, regardless of the religion, is a positive thing. It doesn't matter what form it takes, as long as you are taught right from wrong. I have always had a strong faith in a higher power, so being brought up a Catholic was good for me. I would go to Mass every week at

St Clare's, and I was an altar boy for a while. I still occasionally go to Mass and always feel better for it.

Apart from positive parental influence, I was also lucky that our street was well integrated. There were three Catholic and three Protestant families up our close, and we all got on brilliantly. My best pal, John Hutchison, was a Protestant, and there were never any problems between us. There was Old Firm rivalry, of course, but I watched the 1967 European Cup final in my house with my family, and each time Celtic scored the whole building shook. One man from the nearby Lockdockhart Road lost his son in the Ibrox disaster in 1971, and everybody, Protestant and Catholic, Rangers or Celtic, rallied around him. I remember him coming out of the Masonic lodge at the top of the road and crying for about ten minutes. I had never heard such a cry – it was almost a wailing noise. I felt so sad for him.

But I was well aware that there were fundamental cracks in the community. Being a Catholic involves the home, the church and the school, the last of which has been an issue probably since the education system in Scotland was reorganised at the beginning of the twentieth century. It is still a tricky subject to address. At an early age, I learned that the Catholic schools hated the Protestant (or non-denominational) schools and vice versa, but I didn't understand why. I didn't need to understand why; it was a Glasgow tradition. Rogerfield Primary was built at one end of the park near to where I lived, and my school, St Clare's, was at the other end. There were about twelve football pitches in between the two schools, and at lunchtime – or dinnertime as we called it – the Rogerfield pupils would charge us, and we would charge them. There was no fighting, just charging. If there were more of them on a particular day, we would run away, and if there were more of us, we would chase them.

This scenario was replicated all over Glasgow when two schools were so close to one another, but it was as much to do with ritual as anything else. After school, I would meet up for a game of football with the guys that I had been charging four hours earlier, and we would have a laugh about it. They would say to me, 'That was some charge today from us. You all ran for miles.' And when we had done the charging, I would say to them, 'I noticed you running away, but you shouldn't have bothered. I wasn't going to hit you if I caught you. I would have let you off.' We would then play for hours without another word said about it.

I have heard of Catholic households in which even the name Rangers is a taboo, but that wasn't the case in my house. However, if you attended a Catholic school in Glasgow, you were bound to be a Celtic supporter, and I was no different from all the rest at St Clare's – apart from one. There was one Rangers supporter in our school, and he was treated as an outcast. The 'Lone Ranger', I suppose you could call him. His dad was a Rangers fan, and his mum was a Celtic fan, and he sided with his dad. We would taunt and tease him every now and again: 'You support who? Rangers?' I felt sorry for him, because he was a good wee guy. Who were we to judge him for what team he supported? Nevertheless, we did. Looking back, it must have taken an immense amount of courage for him to go against the flow.

Would I change the education system in Scotland to make it more inclusive? To be honest, I don't know. It's a good question. My own children went to Catholic schools, and they enjoyed the education and moral upbringing. I don't see anything wrong with that. But I do think that segregation has caused problems and continues to foster a sense of division in some communities. We were charging the pupils at the other school just because they were Protestants. That can't be right. Maybe we have to evolve until such times as all Scots children are educated in a uniform way. On a simplistic level, it would surely be cheaper having one building instead of two. But it's a very complex issue.

It would be wrong to say I spent my childhood agonising over religion. Football was my big passion, and Easterhouse in the 1960s was a perfect place to develop that love affair. It was football, football, football. If you didn't like football, there was something wrong with you as far as I was concerned.

The rules were simple. If it was your ball, you were in charge. A decision would often have to be changed to suit the owner of the ball and avoid him ending the game early by walking away in a huff with it held tightly under his arm.

We would go to school early in the morning, pick sides and start a game, run out at playtime to continue, and when we went home we'd quickly change out of our uniforms and scoff our dinners so that we could get back out as quickly as possible. There were always loads of players available, sometimes far too many, and when we played 10–21ers (ten goals marked half-time and twenty-one full-time) on a Sunday there were dozens of bodies fighting for space. I hated boys who were shouted in for their dinner when the score was 20 each or in the balance – that really annoyed me. I like to think that I was more dedicated. I would ask my mum for a piece and jam, and eat it while I ran up the wing.

My first organised games were with St Clare's in the Catholic Schools League when I was around ten. My first proper match was in Spittal, near Rutherglen, against St Mark's on a cold winter's day. My love for trains was to cost me dearly on my debut. I was stuck on the left wing and stopped every time one went past on the Motherwell to Glasgow line – which was every ten minutes or so. In time-honoured fashion, I also got smacked on the thigh by the ball. Mr McDonald, our coach, took me off at half-time, and I just stood there, crying and checking to see how long the Mouldmaster logo would remain on my leg.

My father had no influence on my football career. In fact, he didn't like football. He came to see me play at Glasgow

Green once when I was a schoolboy and got bored. He left at half-time to do some shopping at the Barras then came back to pick me up. I wasn't too bothered. I think that lack of parental pressure can be a good thing for a young boy. I see fathers standing at the side of the park shouting and bawling at their kids, and I get angry at that. The kids get nervous and become frightened to make a mistake, and you can see that they are not enjoying what should be a fun time. Parents should let their children enjoy themselves as I was allowed to do.

Perhaps my dad was simply unimpressed by what he saw. I wasn't the best player in my age group; there were plenty of others better than me. I knew I had skill, but despite all the soup my mother made I was weaker than most of the boys my age. I was picked for the Glasgow Primary School Select, which was encouraging, but I was always a substitute. Also in the squad was a skinny, red-haired boy called Tam from St Mary's in Calton, and he wasn't a bad player.

When I was growing up, football was more about playing than watching. I considered myself a Celtic fan, but I didn't have pictures on the wall or anything like that, and I didn't go to that many games. If I did go to Parkhead, it was with my brother Andrew. My mum didn't let me go to Old Firm games, though, because there was always a lot of fighting afterwards.

I was very fortunate that the Lisbon Lions were on the go when I was growing up. The Lions – who all came from within a 30-mile radius of Parkhead – gave me and people like me hope that we might be able to play for Celtic some day. When I went to games, I would pay special attention to players such as Jimmy Johnstone, Stevie Chalmers, Willie Wallace and Bobby Lennox, and even at a young age I noticed that they all tried to get behind defences, which is something that you hardly ever see nowadays. In particular, I loved watching 'Jinky' Johnstone take on a player and go past him. Willie Henderson of Rangers could also beat a player on the wing and get the crowd cheering, and that's what I wanted to do.

The one Celtic game that I do remember quite vividly was the 1967 European Cup quarter-final against Vojvodina when Billy McNeill scored the winner. It was an incredible game and an incredible atmosphere. I came home that night thinking to myself, 'That was fantastic. I would love to play at Celtic Park, on a pitch like that in front of a such a big crowd.'

I was also an avid Scotland fan, and one of my favourite games to this day is the 3–2 win over England at Wembley in 1967 when Jim McCalliog, Denis Law and Bobby Lennox scored. England were the world champions at that time, but we took over that mantle that day, in our minds at least, and after the game me and my friends went down to the park to replay the famous victory.

Wembley was always a magical place for me. My first visit to the stadium was ten years later when Gordon McQueen scored to give Scotland a 2–1 win. I was playing for St Mirren by that time, but I had no idea that I would be on the bench as part of the Scotland squad just two years later.

But there were more than a few obstacles to overcome before I reached those heady heights. Football gave me the happiest days of a carefree childhood, but like all children I was racked with my own particular anxieties and worries. For one thing, I had a terrible stammer. It came from my mother's side of the family, and it was a horrible affliction, especially for a self-conscious schoolkid. At times, I couldn't speak two words without stuttering, and I hated it. There is nothing more frustrating than people finishing your sentences for you. I especially detested being asked to read in class. There would be a huge groan when Mrs Breslin announced that it was my turn, as my classmates all knew that the passage would take a long, long time to complete. But most of all I hated when it was time for me to go to the speech therapist. My teacher used to take great delight in saying, 'Right, Francis. Time for your clinic.' I felt so humiliated. My self-esteem was at its lowest each time I slipped out the classroom for my therapy.

Some might say that it was character building, but it didn't feel like that at the time. The stammer got me down. I became withdrawn and was unable to mix with other kids as well as I wanted to. I remember coming home from school one night, crying and saying to my dad, 'I wish I could get rid of this stammer.' He was sympathetic but couldn't do anything about it. Thankfully, it went away when I was about 16, but I haven't forgotten how it affected me.

I haven't forgotten how I got my first nickname, either, coming as it did the morning after a Frankenstein film had been shown on television. I normally had long hair, but I got a short back and sides, which showed off my high forehead. When I went to school, all the girls ran away, melodramatically screaming and shouting and calling me 'Frankenstein'. The name quickly stuck, which didn't leave me feeling too good. It thankfully got shortened to 'Stiney', and most people outside my family knew me as that for years afterwards.

As well as coming to terms with personal problems, I also had to grow up during a time when Easterhouse was witnessing a jockeying for position among the six or seven gangs that had been formed. It was not an environment for a Frankenstein lookalike with a stammer, and I duly suffered. No matter how inconspicuous you tried to make yourself, there was always someone 'after you', or rather 'efter ye'. This one was 'efter ye' and that one was 'efter ye', usually people you had never met before, and for no reason.

Due simply to living in Dungeonhill Road, I was bestowed membership of the local gang, the 'Den Toi', whether I wanted to be in it or not. If I found myself in another part of Easterhouse, I would be asked, 'What gang are you in?' I would reply, 'I'm not in a gang. I'm just over for a game of football.'

That wasn't good enough. Invariably, the next question would be, 'Where do you stay?' I would tell them, and they would say, 'That's where the Den Toi come from, and we're efter them.' If I couldn't run away, I would get a doing. Before I knew it, fighting had become a part of daily life.

When I was in primary seven, a new boy came to St Clare's and immediately declared himself to be the best fighter in the school. He found no opposition and was soon throwing his weight around. I scored against his team one day, and he had me up against the wall, choking me and threatening, 'If you score another goal against us, you're getting a doing.' Of course, I did score, and he had me up against the wall again. In a moment of blind panic, I punched him in the face, giving him a black eye. I was literally saved by the bell, which rang at that moment, but he loudly announced to all and sundry that he wanted to fight me after school, up the forest at ten to four, the allocated time for such events. Everyone was laughing at him, which was making things worse for me. I just wanted to say sorry and be pals with him, but he was mortified that he had a black eye and wanted his revenge. I mentally prepared myself for one of the biggest beatings I had ever had. I was terrified, but before the end of the day, one of his pals sent a note over to me saying that he couldn't fight because he had to go to the dentist. It was one of the happiest moments of my life. The relief was immense. He was just as scared as me, and I never had any problems with him after that.

A few years later, I was making my way to St Leonard's Secondary School with my two mates, Peter McCusker and John Shields, when I noticed out of the side of my eye a Lochend Secondary School pupil who was apparently efter me. I wanted to keep walking, but Peter and John, almost gleefully, said I had to face him, even though both of them would have done a runner if they had been in my situation.

We squared up to each other with me trying to conceal the inescapable fact that I had never been so frightened in all my life. I soon heard the immortal words 'Am efter you'. I stammered back, 'A-a-a-a h-h-heard,' thus sounding even more pathetic than I felt. He was acting the big man, saying, 'Well, what are you going to do about it?' Soil my pants was my first thought, but I was so frightened and nervous that when he moved closer I punched him twice before he could get a hit in. Those split seconds seemed like hours, but he then started screaming, 'Leave me, leave me.' I couldn't believe it. I had won. But, of course, my unexpected victory came at a price. Everyone got to know about it, and then all the local neds wanted to fight me.

However, those scrapes pale into insignificance when I recall a really lucky escape I had a few years on. John, Peter and I were walking home one night when we realised that we were being followed by six guys. They were about 50 yards behind us and slowly catching up. We tried to remain calm and not let them see that we were frightened, but that illusion was shattered when we came to John's house and he bolted inside without a word of warning. A few seconds later, Peter said, 'As soon as we get to this next close, Stiney, I'm running through it, up the back and into my house.' I didn't feel much like being left on my own, so I said, 'So am I.' There was no chance of them catching me if I was at full speed, but I was worried that there would be no one to open the door when I reached my house. Quick as a flash, we were through the close and gone our separate ways like two frightened gazelles. I don't even know if they gave chase, but I could hardly catch my breath when I scrambled into my house, relieved that the door was open and my mum was inside.

We later found out that about ten minutes after we had made our getaway, a boy from the top of the scheme had been fatally stabbed in the heart by the same group of guys who had followed us up the road. I was frozen with fear and was extra careful for weeks after that. I realised that being in the wrong place at the wrong time could mean serious trouble. That was the downside of Easterhouse.

Indeed, Glasgow as a whole was continuing to live up to its 'No Mean City' tag. The city had long needed a strong leader and a new initiative to help eradicate its depressing gang culture. Unsurprisingly, a bizarre intervention by crooner Frankie Vaughan in the late 1960s failed to work.

Frankie, one of the great entertainers of his time, played a concert in Glasgow and was apparently appalled at the level and intensity of violence in some parts of the city. He asked for a meeting with gang leaders and appealed for a weapons amnesty. Easterhouse was the place he chose to make his appearance. Television cameras, photographers and reporters turned up to see Frankie, who had a Pied Piper effect on the local youths, who, like me, emerged from all corners of the scheme to see what all the fuss was about.

The whole stage-managed event was pointless. Frankie knew it, and we knew it. It wasn't as if the gangs were going to say, 'Frankie Vaughan wants us to stop fighting, so we will.' The hooligans just wanted to see their faces in the newspapers or on television and paid little heed to the amnesty – they handed in their old swords and kept their new ones at home. The trouble continued.

Sadly, I don't think you will ever stop some young guys wanting to bash each other up. I was in Sauchiehall Street in the summer of 2007, and I saw a gang fight between about 50 young guys, which approximately 25 policemen were unsuccessfully trying to stop. It was worse than anything I had ever witnessed in Easterhouse as a youngster.

2

· ·

TRIBULATIONS, TRIALS AND A MAN CALLED FERGIE

When Frankie made good his escape, local people continued to put their time and effort into more practical solutions to the problems we had in the area. There were always older men, parents and budding coaches willing to put together a football team and register them in one of the numerous leagues that had sprung up all over the city and beyond.

An Under-12s team called Rantic was formed by a guy called John Docherty. The name revealed an attempt to integrate the Catholic and Protestant communities through their respective football teams. (I think even the Celtic fans thought 'Rantic' sounded better than 'Celgers'.) It was an idea that was replicated in other areas of Glasgow, and although it wasn't even a sticking-plaster solution to a deep-rooted problem, it was nevertheless carried out with the best of intentions.

Bobby Russell, who went on to play for Rangers and Motherwell, was one of my teammates at that time. I have always thought that it was fitting in some ways that he went to Ibrox and I ended up at Celtic Park – but on the other hand, maybe it showed that the idea didn't really work.

After a few years, I left to join another team run by a local man. He was a good manager who had lots of time for the boys in the team, but there was one problem: it seemed that he wanted to interfere with us all. The term paedophile was not in widespread use at the time, and to us, in those politically incorrect days, he was simply a poof.

In many ways, he was like the numerous youth coaches in towns and cities all over Scotland who spend all their spare time running football teams. We were in our early teens, and he was in his 30s. Over six feet tall with brown hair, he was just a normal-looking guy. He was bit of a loner, but it was a more innocent time, and my parents trusted him implicitly. They would invite him into our house, and he would tell them that I was going to be a footballer when I grew up. I was one of his favourites, and he had a lot of faith in me as a player. Before his predilection for young boys came to the fore, I was happy enough for him to take me into Glasgow and give me money to play the amusements.

I was as naive as most 14 year olds, and although the first person to show any interest in me sexually was a man, I was blissfully unaware of it at the time. I was in the toilets in Queen Street Station when this middle-aged guy who was standing beside me asked, 'Do you want to come home with me?' I replied, 'What for?' I had no idea why he would want me to go home with him, but something told me that it wasn't right, and I quickly got out of the toilets. It was only later that I realised what had really happened.

I hadn't had a girlfriend by that time. Having a stammer and looking like Frankenstein's monster wasn't a great combination. I thought I had knocked it off when one girl said that she wanted to go out with me and we went round the back of the house for our first kiss. It was an awkward and embarrassing moment. I gave her a cuddle and then manoeuvred myself into position to give her my best shot, but it wasn't like the movies, and she quickly ended our romantic interlude by disappearing into the distance at great speed. My fragile confidence was shattered, and I thought, 'Maybe girls are not for me.'

The episode with the coach was more prolonged. It first came to light when one of the boys told us that he had tried to touch him up. I didn't really believe him at first – until I experienced it for myself. We trained in the local school a couple of times a week, and one night I banged my ankle during a game of fives and needed it looked at. The gym had big storage cupboards, and the coach would make a bed in there, which was meant to be the treatment table. Initially, I didn't think anything of it. As I hobbled over, the other boys were saying, 'You better watch yourself, Stiney,' but I wasn't worried. It was my ankle that was the problem.

Even when he closed the doors and made sure that they were locked tight, I didn't think anything untoward was going on. He told me to lie down on the bed, and then he put a towel over my shorts. I was lying there as if in an operating theatre. He started rubbing my ankle and then slowly moved up my leg to my groin area. My blood ran cold, and my stomach began churning. I said, 'What are you doing? It's my ankle that's sore.' I will always remember his answer. 'I'm just trying to get the blood flowing down your leg to the ankle.' My ankle was the last place he wanted my blood to flow to, and I was worried that he might get his wish. I became frightened. I was naive, but, like the day I was propositioned in the toilets in Queen

Street Station, I knew that something wasn't right. I said, 'It's OK, my ankle is fine now. Let me up.'

He never bothered me again – he simply moved on to some of the others. He would take the whole team to the cinema and turn up with a blanket. At first I wondered, 'Why has he got a blanket at the pictures? Surely it's not cold in the cinema?' But we soon noticed that he would put the blanket over him and one of the players sitting next to him. I would hang back and let my teammates sit down before me so that I could sit by the aisle. I wanted to be as far away from him as possible.

Eventually, we all got wise to him. After one cup final that was particularly brutal, he asked if anyone was injured, and we all said no, preferring to cover up our bruises and limp away. I can only surmise what damage he did before we realised what he was up to.

I don't know why, but we didn't say anything to anyone outside of the team. I didn't dare tell my parents or brothers. It was as if it was my and my teammates' secret shame. We had heard that this sort of thing went on at other teams at that time, but it was just snippets and quiet whispers. I have since met some of the guys who played in the same team as me, but most of them haven't broached the subject.

In 1996, when I read about Jim Torbett and the Celtic Boys Club scandal, my old coach immediately came to mind. I had to hand it to Alan Brazil, who dredged up all that stuff from his past and went looking for the guy who had interfered with him and some of his teammates. It must have taken some bottle to go through with the trial and all the publicity that it engendered. Torbett was convicted of sexually abusing boys under his care, including Brazil, over a seven-year period and was consequently jailed.

There have been other cases over the years of youth coaches interfering with their charges, which is no surprise, really. An underage football team that provides an unlimited supply of young boys is manna from heaven for those types. There have been safeguards put in place recently that attempt to prevent something similar from happening, but for many it has been too late. I was strong enough to say no, but a feeling of guilt still remains. Recently, I met one of my former teammates from that time who confessed that he had been carrying the same secret as me and had suffered at the hands of our former coach.

I don't know where he is these days, or, indeed, if he is still alive. If I'm being honest, I don't hate him. What he did was very wrong, but in other ways he was a nice guy, and he was always good to me, although I'm aware that if I had been abused my feelings would be very different. What has happened is that I have become wary of gay men. It sounds homophobic, but it's just the way I feel. And I can't go into the Queen Street Station toilets any more. I get a shiver down my spine just driving past the place.

I made my escape from my old coach and the Den Toi when we moved to Balornock to be closer to my mum's family. But in some ways it was a case of jumping out of the frying pan and into the fire. My new school, St Augustine's, drew many of its pupils from Maryhill, Possil, Springburn and Milton – four of the toughest areas of Glasgow – and a fair proportion of them wanted to fight the new boy. In an attempt to integrate into my new environment, I joined the school football team, where I played alongside a scrawny-looking guy called Tony Higgins. But that was to no avail. I was in ten fights in the first six weeks. What was going on? Girls weren't interested in me, older men wanted to bugger me and younger boys wanted to batter me.

As a solution to the last of these problems, I decided to stop going to school. I returned for my O levels after about a year away, but I was ill-prepared for the exams. I left school at 15 to make my way in the world, nursing a grievance that my education hadn't been looked after properly.

I messed around for a bit, playing some golf and football, but, of course, I needed money. My first job was as a delivery boy with Barr, dropping off crates of Irn Bru to shops all over Glasgow, but that didn't last long. After a few weeks, I was sacked for stealing, of all things, a Swiss roll.

The driver told me that he supplemented his wages by pinching 20 cigarettes from every shop that we delivered to, then selling them on. When some of the shopkeepers became suspicious, he saw the opportunity for me to take the blame. I got done up like a kipper. He said to me at one shop, 'Take a Swiss roll if you want. Nobody will bother.' When I did, the sneaky bastard told the shopkeeper, who then called the police.

I know I shouldn't have taken it, but I was raging that he had set me up. When I got back to the depot, he told the gaffer that I was to blame for all the thefts that had taken place, and I got sacked on the spot. They made up my wages there and then, and I walked away with a grand total of £5.50 in my pocket. I thought about waiting around to confront the driver, but he was bigger than me, so I decided that he might have only made a bad day worse. Instead, I went to an amusement arcade in Argyle Street and spent every penny I had. I didn't even keep 5p for my bus fare, so I had to walk home that night, which gave me more than enough time to come up with a story for my parents.

However, my sacking was a blessing in disguise, because a few weeks later I started as an apprentice joiner with Glasgow Corporation. Getting a trade was a big thing for a school leaver, and it was eventually the thing that saved me.

I was still keen to become a footballer. My cousin Tommy Hannah asked me to go along to his team, Colston Amateurs from the north side of Glasgow, and I played well enough in my first game to be asked back by their manager Ian French, a lovely man who was to become the single most influential figure in my football life. Quite simply, if it wasn't for him, I would not have become a professional footballer. He had more faith in me than I had in myself.

I did well at Colston. I was enjoying my football, playing at centre-forward and scoring a lot of goals, and after one game Ian said to me, 'I think you could make it as a professional.' I wasn't so sure. I wasn't one of those players who had been courted by lots of clubs. I hadn't been the best in my school, or even the best in my street. But Ian made it his job to put me on the map, and luckily for me he was part of a three-man committee who picked me for a Glasgow amateur select team to go to the 1974 World Cup in West Germany. Archie Stormonth, Bill Toy and Ian were in charge of a dozen or more wide-eyed 18 year olds, and we had a fantastic time in what for most of us was our first trip abroad. We watched an average Brazil side lose 2–0 to Holland, who had the great Johan Cruyff playing. Holland reached the final only to be beaten by the hosts 2–1, but Cruyff confirmed his status as a world-class player. As I came off the bench for the select side in a game against the local German amateur team, I didn't think he and I would be coming up against each other in the future.

When we returned to Glasgow, Ian got me a trial with Clyde, and I played for their second team against Ayr United at Somerset Park. I was hopeless. I was playing against an older, more experienced left-back with a shock of white hair who didn't give me a kick, and, to make things worse, I required stitches above my eye after heading one of their players. The manager handed me £2 for expenses, and when we got back to Glasgow he sent me to hospital to get a tetanus jab. I wasn't asked back, and it was the first of several disappointments. I then went to train with St Roch's, a junior side from the north of Glasgow. Willie O'Neill, who was at Celtic when they won the European Cup, although he didn't play in the final, was the manager. Every training night for about three weeks, I was the first to arrive at the ground, trying to impress him. I was working hard and scoring goals in the bounce matches. I was desperate to get a game, and in my mind I was just as good as any of the St Roch's players.

One week, it emerged that they only had ten players available for the match at the weekend, and I thought, 'Thank God, I'm going to get a game at last.' I could hardly contain my excitement. I was puffing out my chest to make sure Willie could see me, but at a team meeting he said, 'We will just have to go with ten players.'

I couldn't believe what I had heard. I felt my face burning as I walked away, and on the way home I started crying. It was humiliating to think that any team would rather play with ten players than give me a game. He actually believed that having me in the team would be worse than playing with a man short – the ultimate football insult. In the end, I think they got another player, but I vowed never to go back again and decided I was going to give up on football altogether. I've seen Willie around over the years, but I've never spoken to him since. If I had been the manager, perhaps I might not have played me. I was five feet eight inches and slightly built, but then again – ten men!

I told Ian what had happened, and in no time at all he phoned me to tell me that he had fixed me up with an outing with another junior side, Rob Roy. However, I was so frustrated with the way things were going that I didn't want to go through another trial. It's hard to play as a trialist. You have to be selfish and impress when you are on the ball, but you also have to be aware that it is a team game. But Ian was persuasive, so I agreed to go.

On the day, I was decidedly average. I wasn't any better or worse than any of the other Rob Roy players, but in a trial situation you have to stand out. Afterwards, the manager said, 'Don't phone me, I'll phone you.' I waited all week before my mum sat me down and told me that there would be no phone call.

Ian then arranged another trial for me, this time with Kilsyth Rangers in a game against Dunipace, who play up near Cumbernauld. My parents had never watched me at the same time, but for some reason they both turned up that night. I was on the left wing, playing against a tough old right-back, the type that junior football breeds by the dozen, but I skinned him early on and knew then that I had the beating of him all night long. However, the next time I tried to go past him, he flattened me.

My mum started shouting and screaming at him and ran to the side of the pitch with her handbag ready, much to the amusement of the spectators and players. I was mortified. I planned to pick up my clothes and get out of the place without even taking a shower, because I didn't want the other players taking the piss out of me. I was hoping that no one would ever see me again, and I decided that this time I was definitely finished with football.

After the match, I tried to sneak out the back door, but one of the Kilsyth officials grabbed me and told me that they wanted to sign me immediately. Despite my embarrassment, I had apparently played well. They offered me a £25 signing-on fee, £3 a week and, more importantly, about £8 per week in expenses. My wage with the corporation was only £12 a week, so I didn't hesitate, and I quickly settled in to that level of football.

I had had a taste of professional football, albeit at junior level, and I wanted more. Therefore, I was prepared to offer some encouragement to another 'pervert' in order to do so. Only the Kilsyth official with the funny handshake was a Freemason and not a homosexual. When Mr Harrison, who turned out to be a lovely man, shook my hand for the first time, he put his finger down my finger the way Masons do. I thought, 'Oh fuck, another poof.' I was terrified, but I wanted to stay in the Kilsyth team, so I started doing it back to him. Maybe he believed I was a brother, I don't know, but the next thing I heard was that Rangers were interested in me.

It might surprise some people – although not those who know me – but I have never had a problem with Rangers or Rangers fans. I have never said anything derogatory about the club or the supporters, no matter how much stick I was given – and let's face it, I was given plenty over the years during Old Firm games. I always played my best for every team I was a part of, and I would like to think that Rangers supporters, like most other football fans in Scotland, accept that. I often get Rangers fans coming up to me in Glasgow, shaking my hand and saying, 'Frank, you were a good player.' Sometimes they say, 'I didn't like you, Frank, but you were a good player' but that's usually the extent of the flak I get.

Would I have signed for Rangers? The honest answer is yes. Rangers hadn't signed a Catholic for decades when I was starting off my career, and there was a strong anti-Catholic feel to Ibrox and among a lot – but not all – of their fans. But I would have played for them. The only problem would have been at supporters' functions, which players were expected to attend in those days. Hearing songs that include lines such as 'We're up to our knees in Fenian blood' would have been a problem for me, and I'm not sure what I would have done. But, as it turned out, the question was hypothetical. It would have been interesting to see what would have happened if Rangers had followed up their initial interest, but it seemed that once they found out which school I attended they looked elsewhere.

St Mirren, in the First Division at the time, became the beneficiaries, and it was former Rangers player Willie Thornton who tipped off a young, up-and-coming Buddies manager called Alex Ferguson about me. In Ferguson's book *Alex Ferguson: Managing My Life*, he reveals that Thornton told him that Rangers wanted to sign me from Kilsyth Rangers. Thornton then told Fergie, 'He is no use to us, but he is a very good player.' Fergie knew nothing about me, but I was given a trial on Thornton's recommendation. I didn't play that well and afterwards Fergie said, 'I'm not too sure about you, son. Come back for another trial.' I didn't impress much on that occasion, either, but at the behest of St Mirren scout Jack Gilmour I was given a chance until the end of the season. I wasn't going to cost the club much, so they had nothing to lose.

I was already dreaming of life as a professional in the senior ranks, and I wasn't that interested in Kilsyth after I signed for St Mirren. But junior football was an excellent experience, and I would like to see it regain its place in Scottish football. As an apprentice joiner, was I better learning alongside other apprentices or with the tradesmen? The same applies to young footballers. Under-18s and Under-21s should be playing against experienced players. They would learn quicker and pick up all their tricks as well as their trade. These days, you have players at 22 and 23 still waiting to make their debut. It's nonsensical.

I was playing for Kilsyth, training with St Mirren and occasionally making appearances for the Buddies' reserves. I got my first taste of first-team football towards the end of the 1974–75 season. I was 19 when, on 26 April 1975, to be precise, I came on as a substitute against East Stirling at Firs Park, and we lost 5–0. It was the second-last game of the campaign, and it was hardly a glamorous introduction to senior football. The ground was a dump, the dressing-rooms were tiny, the pitch was worse than any of the junior ones I had played on and, of course, it was against Fergie's former club. But I had my foot in the door, and I was happy with the year's contract he handed me before we dispersed for the summer.

I was glad of the break. Apart from my joinery work and training and playing for two teams, I was also working in an ice-cream van at night. My brother and I had rented the van, but he didn't like working weekends, which meant that I would come home from a game on a Saturday, go straight out with the van and then work in it all day Sunday when I should have had my feet up. And it wasn't as if I was seeing the benefits of my labour. When people think about ice-cream vans in Glasgow housing schemes, they think about the 'Ice Cream Wars', the battles between rival factions protecting their lucrative patches, which the media loved to talk about. But I wasn't involved in any ice-cream wars – I wasn't making any money, so nobody needed to be at war with me. We must have had the only van on the road that didn't make a profit, and we soon got rid of it.

That summer, I booked to go to the Isle of Man with my mates, my first holiday without adult supervision, but Fergie wasn't happy about it. The corporation's holidays were set in stone – the Glasgow Fair fortnight – which meant I missed two weeks of pre-season training. I wasn't a drinker normally, but I had a few pints every night as we did what guys did. Old habits die hard, though, and I played football on the beach every day – a Scotland versus England kickabout with anyone who was interested. The games went on for about three hours at a time, and players would come and go during the course of a match. It would go from ten-a-side to fifteen-a-side and back again, and I loved it – it was like Easterhouse with sun and sand.

Fergie was very strict in regard to drinking – as I was later to find out to my cost – and I was wary of coming back and having him find out that I had been hitting the high spots of the Isle of Man. Of course, every player would have been enjoying himself over the summer holidays. It was expected that most would come back a stone or so over their playing weight. But I had already annoyed him by going on holiday, so I didn't want to give him anything else to complain about.

As soon as I walked into training the first time after the summer break, Fergie barked, 'Right, up to the office.' I thought, 'Oh no, he's found out already.' I was scared that I was going to be released or sacked. But he told me that he needed me to play against Reykjavik in a friendly at Love Street in a few days' time. My relief at not being bollocked outweighed my delight.

It was the night of Wednesday, 6 August 1975 that I came to the attention of the St Mirren fans for the first time by scoring four times against the Icelandic side in a 5–3 win. It was, as they say, one of those nights when I could do no wrong. We were losing 1–0 when I picked up the ball, flew past a defender and stuck it into the net for my first St Mirren goal. Three minutes later, I grabbed my second when I got the ball at the edge of the box and fired it into the top corner, and I completed my hat-trick one minute before the interval.

My training on the Isle of Man beaches, which I thought had just been a bit of fun, had stood me in good stead. The much-needed three or four weeks' rest beforehand had also allowed my body to grow. I had been about ten and a half stone at the end of the previous season, and I came back to pre-season training around eleven stone four pounds. I was ahead of everybody on the pitch in terms of fitness and at least half a yard faster than any of the Reykjavik defenders. My fourth came with six minutes to go when most players were dead on their feet. The next day, I was so unknown that most of the papers spelled my name wrong, and I awoke to read headlines such as 'McGarvie Saints' hot shot'.

After the game, Fergie called me up to his office again. He said, 'What have you been doing on holiday? That was brilliant tonight. Report for the first team for the next game.' I'd thought that he was going to sack me a few days earlier, and there I was being drafted into the first-team squad for a League Cup tie against East Fife the following Saturday.

Fergie then put me on the bench against an experienced Bayview side at Love Street. We scored through a Walter

Borthwick penalty after an hour, but we couldn't finish them off. Fergie said to me, 'Go on and get us a goal,' which I did in the 71st minute, and although they pulled one back we were comfortable winners in the end. After a circuitous route, I had arrived in the world of professional football and was part of the St Mirren first-team squad at just 19. Fergie was very complimentary about me, telling the press that I had a lot of talent. I was pleased that he was pleased with me. It wouldn't always be like that.

3

GAMBLING ON GOALS

Alex Ferguson is a legend. He is Scotland's most successful manager and has been knighted for his services to football. Winning numerous championships, cups and European trophies with clubs north and south of the border will ensure his place in the record books. But when I arrived at St Mirren, he was just making his way in the game. He had come from East Stirling, arguably the worst senior club in Scottish football, and had done nothing yet as a manager. He was still better known as a former Rangers centre-forward who had played the game with his elbows.

However, his impact on Love Street cannot be over-estimated. Before Fergie's arrival from Firs Park, crowds at Love Street were low, and there was little if no money to spend on players, but he refused to let that get him down, and his infectious enthusiasm spread from the dressing-room throughout the whole town.

Much of Fergie's reputation as a top-class manager has been forged on bringing good young players through the ranks and not being afraid of giving them first-team experience. At Aberdeen, he successfully introduced youngsters such as Neale Cooper, Neil Simpson and Eric Black, and at Old Trafford he drafted in, to name but a few, David Beckham, Ryan Giggs and Paul Scholes. He was equally successful with the same bold strategy at St Mirrren. Older players such as Walter Borthwick, John Young and Donny McDowall were gradually phased out and in came Billy Stark, Tony Fitzpatrick and me. Tony was captain by the time he was about 20.

I knew I would be given a chance if I showed I was good enough at Love Street, but, to his credit, Fergie knew that there was more to life than being a footballer. I signed as a part-time player, and when I asked him what I should do about my trade as a joiner he told me to stay on, complete my time and get my City and Guilds qualification. It was probably the best bit of advice he ever gave me. Fergie came from a working-class background in Govan and had been an apprentice toolmaker with a couple of firms based in the Hillington Industrial Estate in Glasgow. He knew all about the pitfalls of football. What would I have done if I had broken my leg and couldn't play again? It would have been easy for him to tell me to go full-time in order to speed up my development, but he did the right thing by me, and I've always admired him for that.

But what Fergie couldn't do was influence my growing predilection for gambling. I had developed an interest in cards while at school. When I was 15, I did a Sunday morning paper round in Balornock, and on a Sunday afternoon I would go to my friend Drew McCafferty's house to play in a card school that assembled every week. I would never leave his house with any money and was therefore effectively working for nothing.

However, I didn't gamble much from the age of 16, when I lost my first wage in the amusement arcade, until I was about 18. I then got involved in card schools again at lunchtimes on the building sites, and I became intrigued by horse racing. When I came to the horse-racing section of the newspaper, I wondered how anyone could understand it. It seemed so complicated. It still does. But I won two or three quid playing cards one day, and a guy on the site asked me if I wanted to 'put a line on'. I grabbed the newspaper as if I knew what I was talking about, picked the names of four horses that I liked, gave him 50p and told him to put a line on for me – whatever that meant. I forgot about it for the rest of the day.

The next morning, I asked him how I had got on, and he told me that they had all won. After lunch, he came over to me and said, 'There's £8 for you.' I couldn't believe it. I was only earning about £12 a week at the time. That was me hooked on horses. Maybe it would have been different if I had lost, but over the next few days, with beginner's luck, I kept winning with doubles and trebles. It seemed like easy money. It was great. In fact, at that point, life was great. I was a professional footballer for St Mirren and enjoying my joinery work. I was young, single, had plenty of money and not a care in the world.

But then came the next stage of my gambling career when I started to actually go to bookies' shops. Bookmakers had only been made legal in the early 1960s. Before then, they were hidden up closes, or bookies' runners stood at street corners taking bets, literally having to run at times when the police came. The government realised that they couldn't control the increasing desire to gamble, so they legalised the industry and taxed it. It's funny how many illegal practices are suddenly legalised if the government can make money from them.

Initially, bookies' premises were small, horrible and smoky places, and the owners were prevented from having a window at the front of the shop in case 'innocent' people were corrupted on walking past. There were few televised races. A live commentary of a race would come from the track via a Tannoy stuck up in the corner of the shop. It was the most peculiar thing, people standing transfixed, staring at a Tannoy, waiting on good news.

Horse racing slowly invaded my everyday life. On one occasion, I had a fancy for a horse called Decent Fellow that was running at Cheltenham, a race meeting I would come to love. I had a tenner on at 7–2, my biggest bet to date. I told my mum, 'If this wins, I'll give you £20,' which meant that she would get more than me if I won. But that is often the case. Gamblers don't necessarily want to win money so that they can buy something or do something positive with their winnings; the fun is often in being able to throw their winnings around.

I was in an elderly woman's house fixing locks on her doors as the race was about to begin. I asked her if she could put the television on so that I could watch it. She said, 'I want these locks put on, son, and anyway I don't think you should be watching horse racing at your age.' I tried a more tactful approach and asked her again nicely, 'If you could put the television on for five minutes, I would be very grateful,' so she relented, and I downed tools to see how my horse fared.

The race was far too close for my liking, but Decent Fellow won by half a length, and I shouted the house down as it came through in the final few furlongs. The buzz was incredible – a buzz that only a gambler will know. When I was leaving, the woman said, 'Do you know something, son? You've got a problem with gambling.' I walked away thinking, 'I've got a problem with gambling? I've just won three and a half weeks' wages. Where's the problem there?' After I collected my winnings, I gave my mum the £20 I had promised. The unbelievable excitement of seeing a horse I had backed winning was more than enough for me.

Gambling on football was a different matter altogether. Despite being a footballer, I didn't bother with the fixed-odds football coupons that were becoming more and more popular. One of the main reasons I stayed away from betting on games came as a result of a fright I got as a young player when I tipped St Mirren to beat Partick Thistle just at the end of my first full season at Love Street. The irony was that I didn't even put any money on us that day.

I was becoming a minor celebrity at work and used to have a lot of banter with the other workers, mostly Celtic and Rangers fans. They loved the fact that there was a footballer working with them, so I was the centre of attention. The guys would say to me, 'Who do you fancy this week, Frank?' I would reply that this team were worth a bet or that this team were hopeless, but I would never back my own tips.

We were up against Thistle in the Spring Cup at Firhill on 10 April 1976, and I had heard that they were only playing their second team against us. They had beaten us three times that season, so we were around 6–1 to win, which I thought was a terrific price. I would have said that 1–3 were more realistic odds. I didn't think we could get beaten, so I went into work and, with far too much youthful bravado, bellowed out to all who would listen, 'Boys, I've got your holiday money sorted out,' and waited for them to bite. I didn't have to wait long. They were all saying, 'What do you mean you've got our holiday money sorted out?' I was milking it and said, 'Don't worry. You'll be able to take the wife and weans away for a fortnight, and you'll have all your spending money. I've got a team on Saturday that can't get beat, and they are an unbelievable price.' At first, I didn't tell them who it was. I was enjoying the feeling of importance.

I didn't reveal my hot tip until the Thursday when we all got paid, because that's when the guys would fill out their weekend coupons, putting down a stake of maybe one or two pounds. When Thursday arrived, I gathered the guys round and explained that there was no way on God's green earth that St Mirren could get beaten by Partick Thistle. It just couldn't happen, and if they wanted easy money, then they should take my word for it or never ask me for a tip again. As they had to pick two other teams to complete the minimum football bet of a treble, I advised them that they should bet on us and two odds-on shots and make themselves as much money as they wanted.

But I had over-egged the pudding. What had started as a joke grew out of control. Word got around about the game that was going to make everyone a fortune, even to the Pollok Rent Office, situated next door. Easterhouse's very own Frankenstein had created another monster. I was informed that some guys were putting £30 and £40 on, which was three and four weeks' wages. And one of the guys who had bought into my bragging was the resident psychopath who worked in the store room. He was about six feet four inches and built to match. Like most of the corporation employees, I was terrified of him and for good reason. I was there the day that he caught a guy stealing from the store. During the course of a savage beating, he broke the culprit's arm − all for a hammer that cost less than £1. I had been sick looking at the guy's twisted limb as he lay prostrate following his punishment beating. But not as sick as I was when I heard our not-so-friendly psycho had joined the syndicate and had put £60 on St Mirren to win, all on my say-so.

My bluff had been called big time. I realised what was happening and began backtracking. I was going around my colleagues saying, 'I meant for you to put £1 or £2 on, that's all.' But the smell of pound notes was in the air, and my co-workers were understandably saying to me, 'What do you mean? You told us that St Mirren would get us our holiday money. We need to put on more than a couple of quid.' My guts churned a little bit more.

People were enquiring about complimentary tickets and admission prices for the match, but I didn't want anyone to go. I didn't want to go myself. The night before the game brought little sleep. Was a broken arm as sore as it looked? When I came out to warm up at Firhill, there was a crowd from my work and a representation from the Pollok Rent Office all sitting next to each other in the main stand, shouting down at me and waving. My heart sank further.

When I discovered that Thistle were playing most of their first-team players, I must have gone pale. In the dressing-room, Fergie said to me, 'Are you all right? You don't look well.' I replied, 'I'm fine gaffer,' but I was feeling sick. I didn't want to play. I wanted to be anywhere else in the world except Firhill. I vowed that, regardless of the result, I would never tip my team again, a promise that was reinforced in the ninth minute when one of their players drove the ball into the top corner from about twenty yards out.

As we trudged back to take the centre, my mind was all over the place. I was thinking of excuses and explanations, but mostly I was thinking about the mad storeman. I considered getting a train to London after the game and staying off work for a week until it all cooled off.

It might have been the sheer terror I was feeling that inspired me to score the equaliser a minute later. Relief surged through me as I headed Billy Stark's cross past Alan Rough. I was running on a mixture of adrenalin and fear when I put us ahead just before the interval. What a state to be in. Half-time brought a measure of calm, but my teammates were wondering why I was so keen to win a Spring Cup game. If they had only known. I set up Tony Fitzpatrick to score a third with 20 minutes to go, and I could relax until the final whistle. I had fulfilled my side of the bargain.

The other two odds-on shots came up, and everyone was happy, nobody more so than me, even though I didn't make a penny. On the Monday, I was paraded around the workshop on the shoulders of a couple of tradesmen. Everybody had their holiday money, but I never again told anyone to bet on my team. It was a lesson worth learning. Trying to play under the pressure of winning was difficult enough without telling people that betting on your team would make them easy money.

I don't believe there is any harm in betting on your own side to win. On the one occasion I did bet on football during my career, I put £10 on St Mirren at 14–1 before the start of the 1976–77 season to win the First Division, but given that it wouldn't pay out for such a long time it didn't really affect me on a match-by-match basis, and I didn't really bother about it until I picked up my winnings.

I was getting on fine with Fergie at that time, but there were plenty of occasions – and I mean plenty – when my admiration lapsed. His famous 'hairdryer treatment', I believe, was tested out on me and the rest of the St Mirren players long before he turned it into an art form at Aberdeen and Manchester United. Even for an Easterhouse boy, some of the language he used seemed a bit industrial. I hated half-time talks when we weren't playing well and the bollockings at the end of games when he wasn't happy. He would throw cups, glasses and tumblers at us, but he would aim at the wall above you so that the glass and broken porcelain would fall on our heads. In his book, he admitted to smashing a bottle of Coke above the heads of a few players at Love Street and watching as the fizzy drink rolled down the walls. I should know. I was one of those players, and he was going off on one about his pet hate: players drinking too much. Fergie was of the opinion that too much alcohol was the scourge of any team, and he famously brought an end to the drinking culture at Old Trafford before leading United to unprecedented success.

After a slow start to his managerial career at Love Street,

Fergie's methods began to pay dividends, although he was helped when we scraped into the new-look First Division as part of an overall restructuring of the game at the end of the 1974–75 season. Instead of two leagues of eighteen, there would be a Premier League consisting of the top ten finishers in 1974–75. The new First Division would consist of the bottom eight from the old eighteen-team First Division and the top six from the old Second Division. We finished fifth, and aimed to consolidate in our first season in the new division as Fergie began to mould his own side. At the end of the 1975–76 season, in which we had been no great shakes, we were offered an unbelievable trip to Barbados, French Guiana and Surinam on a three-week tour that I almost managed to miss due to my big mouth.

I gave Fergie a mouthful after I had been substituted in one game. He just stared at me. He hated anybody giving him stick, especially when all the fans were watching. But there I was, playing in only my first full season, giving it to him between the eyes in a fit of rage. I went straight in the dressing-room, and his assistant Davie Provan came in behind me and said, 'Calm down. He's just wanting to rest you.' Fergie didn't speak to me for the next three weeks, although he continued to play me. Despite my continued participation in matches, I sensed something was up. I knew he wouldn't let it go, and after a few days I was wishing that he had just bollocked me right after the game. At least that would have been the end of it. But Fergie had a more appropriate punishment lined up for me.

The list of those who were going to Barbados was posted, and my name wasn't on it. At first, I thought it was just a mistake. I looked up and down the sheet of paper about five times, but then it dawned on me why I wasn't included.

I was told that I had to apologise sincerely to the gaffer or I wasn't going on tour. But I wouldn't apologise. I was too stubborn. The impasse went on until the end of the season, when I still hadn't apologised. The other players were loving it, winding me up as the days went by, talking about how much sun they would enjoy and how much fun they would have while I was left behind. I pretended that I wasn't bothered, but I knew that Fergie had to win or I would not be going anywhere.

At the club's Player of the Year night, I decided that I would swallow my pride and apologise. The other players were saying, 'Right, Frank. There he is alone, up you go now.' I made dummy run after dummy run. Eventually, when I confronted him and apologised, he ignored me. I went back to my seat and told our physio Ricky Macfarlane, Eddie McDonald, who was one of our coaches, and Tony Fitzpatrick that I had been blanked by Fergie, and they fell about laughing. However, later on that night, Ricky, who subsequently also coached and managed St Mirren, whispered in my ear, 'You're going to Barbados. Don't worry.' It was all a game to Fergie.

It was while we were on tour that I played alongside Fergie. He had finished playing by that time, but he was still reasonably fit, and he always played in the game in training. But the Ferguson–McGarvey partnership lasted only ten minutes before he was sent off!

Fergie's version of his dismissal differs from mine. In his book, he said he wasn't very happy about Robert Torrance getting a hard time from their centre-half, and he came on after half-time to sort him out with his famous elbows. However, from what I remember, Fergie slipped a great ball to me, and the referee, a big blond-haired guy, blew for offside. Fergie said, 'For fuck's sake. He was onside.' The referee said, 'What's your name, sonny?' Fergie replied, 'You're not fucking booking me, are you? The referee said, 'Did you swear again? Off you go.' We ended up getting beat with ten men.

One thing we did agree on was his desire not to let the press find out. The only thing he said to the players after the game

– very slowly for effect – was, 'Don't tell anybody I was sent off.' That's all he was worried about.

Notwithstanding our manager being sent off, the tour was a success. We all got to know each other better and developed a strong team bond. Consequently, by the start of the 1976–77 season, St Mirren's centenary year, we were well placed to make a bid for promotion from the First Division. Four of us were involved with the Scotland Under-21 squad – Bobby Reid, Tony Fitzpatrick, Billy Stark and me – which was quite a compliment to a club not in the top-flight. Jackie Copland was brought in to add experience to our defence, and we had other good players, such as Lex Richardson and Robert Torrance.

We hinted at what we were capable of when we beat Rangers 2–0 in a pre-season friendly at Love Street, and the two goals I scored that day did me no harm. Fergie was certainly happy enough with my form. In November, after we had beaten Arbroath 3–0 to go top of the table, he told the press that I was the best winger in the First Division, even better than a guy coming through at Clydebank called Davie Cooper.

We were still top of the table at the turn of the year, our crowds were going up and people really took notice when we beat Premier League side Dundee United 4–1 in the third round of the Scottish Cup at Love Street in front of 19,000 fans. Imagine St Mirren getting 19,000 for any game these days, even if Love Street could accommodate that many people. But Fergie had captured the imagination of the Paisley public. During the season, we drew crowds of 10,000 to Love Street for games against Greenock Morton, Clydebank and Dundee. Fergie was also becoming a dab hand at mind games. Before the United match, he said to me, 'I was talking to Jim McLean, and he said you were hopeless.' I swallowed it, hook, line and sinker, and I ran the United defence ragged.

When we were drawn against another Premier League side in the next round – this time Motherwell at Fir Park – we took over 10,000 fans with us. Reports estimated the crowd at over 26,000, and there were thousands locked out at kick-off. In addition to a larger than usual home support, thousands of neutrals turned up, and it was a throw-back to the glory days of post-war football in Scotland when terraces were regularly packed. The game itself didn't quite turn out to be the classic that it had promised, but I put all the blame for that on Motherwell manager Willie McLean.

McLean brothers Jim and Tommy are two men generally associated with the more graceful side of the game. Willie must have been born with a different set of genes. His tactics seemed to be simple and easy to understand: kick fuck out of them. To their credit, the Motherwell players followed his instructions to the letter. In Peter Millar, Stuart McLaren and Gregor Stevens, they had in my opinion three of the dirtiest players in Scotland on their books, and if we weren't aware of that before the game, we certainly were afterwards, as we limped out of Fir Park following a 2–1 defeat.

Fergie was raging about their tactics and complained so much to referee Ian Foote that he was reported to the SFA. Our boss had a point. As I saw it, Foote let them away with murder from the second he blew his whistle to start the game. After five minutes, there were three St Mirren players lying injured on the ground after crunching tackles, and we had to ask the Motherwell physio to come on to help treat them. It didn't get much easier for the rest of the afternoon. It was goalless at half-time, and although I scored for us after the break, Vic Davidson's goal and Willie Pettigrew's penalty took them through to the next round.

Fergie told me after the game that he wanted to see me at Love Street at ten o'clock on the Sunday morning. I had scored at Fir Park, so as far as I was concerned he couldn't complain about my contribution. I had heard that Arsenal and Ajax wanted to buy me, so I thought that there might be some movement on that front. Did I fancy Amsterdam or London? Maybe another team had made an offer for me. I even flirted with the possibility that he was about to give me a rise.

I drove in to Love Street the next day and went upstairs to Fergie's office. Before I could get the pleasantries over with, he said, 'I've been told that you were drinking in the Waterloo Bar in Glasgow the night before the game.' I was stunned. He claims in his book that I pled guilty to the accusation and had to apologise, but that is simply not true. I hardly drank, and never before games, and I told him that. Pauline, my wife to be, worked in the pub, and I explained that I had been there to pick her up. I then said that whoever had claimed to have seen me drunk was a liar, and we started arguing. Fergie picked up a set of keys from his desk and threw them at me, aiming to miss as usual. I pointed behind him and said, 'If those keys had hit my head, you were out that windae.'

He screamed, 'What? You'll put me out the windae?' He then came after me. I knew he would have battered me, so I bolted along the corridor and down the rickety old stairs. He stopped, and I heard him shouting, 'Never come back here again.' I shouted back, 'I'll never play for you again anyway, and don't bother phoning me either.' It wasn't the most mature exchange of views.

I had driven to Love Street contemplating the possibility of a move to London or the Continent and returned home banned from the club and with the manager threatening not to let me play football again. He'd wanted to send a message to all the players that there was to be no drinking at the club, because there were a few boozers in the St Mirren dressing-room at that time. But he had picked on the wrong player.

He phoned up a few times, and we eventually made up on the morning before a crucial home game against Clydebank the following week. The Bankies were one of our main challengers for the title, and victory for us would virtually end their interest and put us on the way to the championship. It wasn't the time to wrongly discipline your top scorer, and Fergie knew that.

Promotion to the Premier League meant a lot of money to St Mirren, so Fergie was under pressure to get me back in whether he wanted to or not. He said in his book that he could have put me out of the game at that juncture, which is nonsense. I was worth more money to St Mirren at that time than Fergie was. The club could have got £250,000 for me – they couldn't have got that for him – and, as was shown later, the board were split with regard to support for their manager. If St Mirren had missed out on promotion because Fergie had wanted to teach me a lesson, then I know who would have been out of the door first. Nevertheless, I was disappointed to read the dismissive way in which he wrote that he could have frozen me out. I was a football man, the same as him. Why would that have even crossed his mind?

In the event, we beat Clydebank 3–1, and I got plenty of plaudits for scoring the third after Derek Hyslop and Bobby Reid had given us a 2–0 lead. Billy McColl pulled a goal back from a Davie Cooper free-kick. The win made us hot favourites for the title, and after the game Fergie and I were cuddling. Football is like that. The press reported that I had been a doubt for the game due to an injury I had picked up at Fir Park the week earlier. If only they'd known.

The game that actually won us the First Division championship was on 19 April against Dundee at Dens Park. We blew them away that night, and I scored a hat-trick in a memorable 4–0 win, adding a second-half double to the goals Billy Stark and I had scored just before the break. I also picked up £150 for my £10 bet, which was an added bonus. Fergie was extra pleased because Davie White, who was Rangers manager when he was forced out of Ibrox, was by then the Dundee boss. We had won twenty-five, drawn twelve and lost only two. We ended up four points ahead of Clydebank, with Dundee in third place, eleven points behind us. St Mirren were worthy champions, and I was looking forward to our first season in the Premier League.

4

LEAVING PAISLEY
FOR PAISLEY

S tepping up to the Premier League was always going to be difficult for St Mirren, regardless of the young talent Alex Ferguson had at his disposal. But although the team struggled for most of the season, my form was good. After taking so long to get started, my career was up and running.

September was a good month for me. A goal against Kilmarnock in the League Cup at Love Street was followed by another in a 3–0 home win against Motherwell. I enjoyed reading the rave reviews I was getting in the press. I was selected for the Scotland Under-21 team and played in France with players such as George Burley, Arthur Albiston and John Wark. I then featured against Czechoslovakia in an Under-21 European Championship tournament, and I felt I held my own alongside teammates who were at some of the biggest clubs in the country. I was subsequently named by Scotland manager Ally MacLeod in a squad of 40 for the 1978 World Cup in Argentina, even though I didn't make the final 22. A double against Rangers in a cracking 3–3 draw at Love Street on 17 September was another milestone for me. That was what I was all about: big names and big crowds.

It was heady stuff for a youngster, and one of my greatest thrills at that time was being on the same pitch as George Best, who was playing for Fulham when we were drawn against them in the Anglo-Scottish Cup. We drew 1–1 at Craven Cottage, and I missed a penalty, but it was in the return game at Love Street, on Monday, 26 September, that I had my own personal battle with the great man.

Around 9,000 fans turned up, most of them to see Best, and although he was coming to the end of his career and his pace and mobility were on the wane he still had all the skills. His passing, in particular, was sublime. However, I knew I was in for a good night after I put us ahead with only 90 seconds on the clock. A goal apiece after that took us to the interval ahead, and Saints supporters thought that it was all over after the break when I scored from the penalty spot.

But Fulham were up for a battle, and John Mitchell, who had shot the London club into the 1975 FA Cup final, pulled a goal back and then set up Best for an equaliser. Extra time looked certain, but we scored two goals in the final few minutes to take us into the semi-finals of the competition.

I came off the park raving about Best. A couple of encounters with him during the game had put me in my place and showed me how far I had to go in the game. I had watched him carefully in the first half and thought that I knew what he would do if I tackled him. Twice I moved back to try and take the ball off him, but even though I thought I knew what he was going to do, he still outfoxed me with a shrug of the shoulders and his quick feet. He was a genius. I was more than glad to scamper back up to the centre-forward position and leave someone else to deal with him. But the headline the next day that screamed 'Saint Frank Matches Magic of Best' gave me a huge lift, and I conveniently put his lessons to the back of my mind.

To be honest, I was full of myself at that time. An ever-increasing number of English clubs were beginning to show an interest in me. There was no transfer window then, so players could move at any time during the season, and it seemed as though I was being linked to a different club every week. I was quoted in one paper as saying, 'I wish all these English clubs would shut up and let me get on with it. These big-money reports are getting me down.' There was an element of truth in that, because I was enjoying life at St Mirren. The team was set up to attack, and I was getting plenty of chances to shine. Many newly promoted clubs change their style to a more defensive system, and it is usually the strikers who suffer, forced to survive on scraps, especially away from home. But Fergie encouraged us to play football at all times. We played to win every game, even when we travelled to Ibrox and Parkhead.

It wasn't just me who enticed the scouts to Paisley. Our intrepid boss told the press that he had knocked back four bids from English clubs for his players. He had a go at Aston Villa for sniffing around Tony Fitzpatrick, while Liverpool were rumoured to be keeping an eye on Bobby Reid. Newcastle United were reportedly set to make a bid for me, while Arsenal said that they would offer a record fee for my services. Fergie dismissed the Gunners' interest, but he knew that he couldn't keep us all indefinitely and he was prepared to 'talk business at the end of the season'. There were even rumours of my fee – generally accepted to be around the £250,000 mark – going towards rebuilding the main stand at Love Street.

I was still a St Mirren player when I met my wife Pauline

in a Glasgow pub. She was with a friend and gave me a smile. We quickly got talking, and I discovered that she lived in Cranhill, which was not too far from Easterhouse or Balornock. I plucked up the courage to ask her out, and that was the start of the relationship. We were soon engaged, although I worried about her health. She didn't have a 21st birthday party, as she was in Ruchill Hospital for two weeks. But I had fallen in love with her. We were a close couple who enjoyed spending time with each other, and I was sure that we could overcome any problems we would encounter. Pauline recovered from her illness, and we married on 29 July 1978 when I was just 22 years old, which, in hindsight, was very young. We set up house together, and like all starry-eyed newly-weds, we looked forward to a long and happy life together.

I didn't hide my fledgling gambling career from Pauline, and it didn't seem to be a problem for her at that time. I had slipped into a little routine. I would nip to the local bookie's after training and put on a £2.20 Yankee (a wager consisting of 11 separate bets). I was quite happy with that for the rest of the day. Many other players and managers did the same. Bookmakers, snooker halls, golf courses and pubs – to a greater or lesser extent – all benefited from the short working life of a footballer.

Around that time, Fergie changed training to the afternoon and got us all part-time jobs in the morning. I was with a glazing firm, and being busy in the afternoons helped to keep me out of the bookie's, for a while anyway.

Although I was more than pleased with my personal form, inconsistency was costing us, and after Christmas we struggled to steer clear of the relegation zone, even with the addition of new recruit Jimmy Bone, an experienced striker who turned out to be one of Fergie's last signings. We had been knocked out of the quarter-finals of the League Cup by Celtic and had lost to Kilmarnock in the third round of the Scottish Cup. But we drew 3–3 with Celtic in the league, which showed our true potential. However, we couldn't put a run of results together. Luckily enough for us, Ayr United and Clydebank were struggling just as much as we were that season.

The day after my 22nd birthday, we travelled to play Ayr United at Somerset Park, knowing that if we won the game, they were almost certainly down. We had only won once since Christmas Eve, when we had beaten Clydebank 2–0 at Love Street, so we weren't exactly going into the game on a high. However, we picked a good day to return to form.

Although we were giving them a pasting, all the good chances were falling to Jimmy, who wasn't having one of his most productive afternoons. Just before the interval, he was presented with an open goal from a yard out and missed the target. The rest of the players were cracking up, as we could see our Premier League status disappearing. In addition to our profligacy, their young keeper Ian McGiffen, who was deputising for Hugh Sproat, was playing the game of his life, and it looked like we would have to settle for a draw.

We pounded them towards the end of the game, and with three minutes to go I grabbed the crucial winner when I squeezed the ball in from a tight angle. The Saints players, fans and backroom staff went crazy. Fergie was hugging Tony Fitzpatrick as if we had won the league instead of simply taking a step to staying in it. Ayr were five points behind us, and with only one game in hand they could not make up the gap in the end.

When we got back to the dressing-room, we discovered that someone had broken in and stolen all the players' money. Fergie took control right away, telling us that the club would reimburse us and ask Ayr to settle the bill later. He started taking a note of how much we had all lost. Lex replied that he'd lost £2, Tony £2.75 and Bobby Reid £3.75. I had lost a couple of quid as well, but when he said, 'Frank?' I quickly replied, 'I've lost £95.50.' Fergie choked and said, 'What? Why the fuck did you have all that money on you?' I replied, 'I had a wee win in the bookie's.' The other players were all turning away, trying not to laugh. He gave me more than the rest of the team put together. We also all got a cheque from Ayr United a few days later for the same amount. It was a nice little bonus for avoiding relegation. St Mirren would get their money back from me, and some more, soon enough.

My confidence was sky-high as we approached the final weeks of the season. I scored one of my best goals ever in a 3–0 win over Hibs at Love Street, an overhead kick which went in off the post. The *Sunday Post* reporter waxed lyrical: 'For sheer magic and class, Frank McGarvey's goal took some beating.' I lapped it all up. I didn't want the season to end, but it finished with a 3–1 home win over Celtic, who had nothing to play for by that point. We had beaten Celtic three times and drawn with them once in the league, and I had scored three times. I also scored three times in the games against Rangers, although we'd registered just two draws.

We survived our first season in the Premier League with a little to spare, finishing in eighth place, six points ahead of Ayr United and eleven ahead of Clydebank, both of whom were relegated. I had scored 19 goals in total for a team that hadn't challenged for honours. Nobody had to tell me my worth, although I knew that I had Fergie to thank for what I had achieved.

Therefore, it was like a death in the family when I found out that Fergie had been sacked. Tony Fitzpatrick, Billy Stark and I were devastated. We couldn't understand it. We had survived a tough opening season in the top-flight, and we were set to make the next step up. All the players had ultimate confidence in the manager, and I believe Fergie could have won the Premier League within two years if he had been allowed to keep all his players and bring in a bit more experience. The Old Firm were there for the taking – we had proved that – and Dundee United were still developing under Jim McLean. There was no one club head and shoulders above the rest.

None of the directors gave us an explanation for their decision. We read about it in the papers, and there was a lot of talk about problems over Fergie's expenses, but that turned out to be rubbish. It was simply a monumental mistake, probably one of the worst decisions ever made by a football board. Fergie made St Mirren a lot of money by taking them into the Premier League, and he had accumulated a set of young players who were worth a fortune to the club, but because of boardroom politics he was forced out.

The chairman, Willie Todd, called a meeting and told the players that the board had someone from the south of England coming up to take over. We did not have a clue who it could be, but we certainly wouldn't have picked Jim Clunie out of a line-up. He was the polar opposite of our recently departed boss. While Fergie always wanted us to attack, Clunie, who had been Lawrie McMenemy's assistant at Southampton, was much more defence minded. I was played wide and asked to chase the full-backs. That wasn't my game, and I quickly became fed up. The atmosphere around Love Street changed markedly, but not for the better.

I wasn't doing myself any favours, as I found myself spending more and more time in the bookie's. Once I went in to put on my first bet of the day, I couldn't get back out again. Winning or losing, I would struggle to force myself out of the door before closing time. My knowledge of horses hadn't increased. Indeed, I still know nothing about horses, and I will never ever know anything about them. The bookies will never get a better animal to run for them. The same horse that can leave a field trailing in its wake in one race can look as if it's two men dressed up in a pantomime horse outfit the next time out – or when I put money on it.

One day in a particularly dingy Paisley bookie's, I managed to get a four-horse accumulator to come in. My winnings worked out at £1,900, an absolute fortune in the late 1970s. However, my delirium soon turned to despair. Unfortunately, I hadn't noticed a sign in the shop that declared the maximum payout to be £500. That was an old trick of the bookies, who wanted to minimise their risks. Your average punter didn't realise it until he went to collect a big payout. Given the money I had donated to this bookie's shop, I was raging that they wouldn't stump up. To rub salt in my wounds, they then took £50 off in tax. Even when I won I lost.

The 1978–79 season got off to a good start when we won the first competitive match of the campaign with a one-goal win at Ibrox thanks to a late strike by Bobby Torrance. That result didn't go down too well with the Rangers fans, who had seen former captain John Greig installed as their new manager after Jock Wallace had left under mysterious circumstances. I was getting used to playing against the best clubs in the country, but there were only two players whom I was wary of: Derek Johnstone and Joe Harper. I was a totally different type of striker, but I admired their qualities. Both players could score goals from nothing and at any time in the game, whether they were playing well or not. Harper, small and stocky, was a tremendous penalty-box centre-forward for Hibs and Aberdeen, although he wasn't so successful at Everton. Johnstone was probably the best player in the air who I ever played against, and in the run-up to the 1978 World Cup finals in Argentina he was, as they say these days, scoring for fun. I never understood why he wanted to play at centre-half, because apart from being good in the air he had no real defensive qualities, and I always fancied my chances when I came up against him.

I scored a first-half hat-trick in a 5–1 win over Berwick Rangers in the League Cup at the start of September while playing against their player–manager Dave Smith, the former Rangers sweeper. Afterwards, Jim Clunie compared me to Denis Law, a childhood hero of mine. I was flattered but humble enough to say, 'I have a bit to go to be in Denis Law's class, although I hope to score as many important goals as he did.' I'm not sure I meant it at the time. I was beginning to act more like another childhood hero of mine, Muhammad Ali, whom I admired for his absolute confidence in his own ability.

Brighton manager Alan Mullery joined the race to sign me, as did Lawrie McMenemy at Southampton. The following month, PSV Eindhoven, who were knocked out of the European Cup by Rangers that season, entered the fray. Previously, I had been ambivalent about all the interest and hadn't allowed it to interfere with my game, but for the first time since I had joined the club I considered the possibility of moving on. I missed the guiding hand of Fergie. Both of us wanted the same out of the game, and he had been good for me. Early in December 1978, I tried to force St Mirren's hand by asking for a transfer. I told the press that I was 'unhappy with my role in the team and . . . could play better in front of bigger crowds'. It all turned a bit sour. One newspaper revealed that at £15,000 a year, I was one of the highest-paid players in Scotland. I suspect that the information was leaked by someone at the club, but if it was, they had exaggerated the figure. I wasn't earning quite as much as that, but well over £10,000 a year, which wasn't bad for any footballer in Scotland at that time.

There was a cartoon in the *Daily Record* of a punter turning up at Love Street with his boots over his shoulders and saying, 'For £15,000, can I have a transfer in?' St Mirren had some of the best players in Scotland on the books, and Fergie had been shrewd enough to keep them happy. He accepted that some players were more important than others. Bobby, Tony and I were on £150 per week at the time plus a double bonus, which I think was around £60. When I went to Celtic in 1980, the highest paid players at Parkhead, Davie Provan and Roy Aitken, were on £150 a week.

Of course, we couldn't tell the other players what we were earning or that we were on a double bonus. That would have caused havoc. And sure enough, there was a lot of tension in the dressing-room when the stories came out in the papers. But I wasn't embarrassed. I thought I was worth it, because St Mirren were knocking back bids of £250,000 for me. The three of us weren't going to say no to the offer of a good wage and a double bonus. They were always going to get their money back for Tony and me, at least, so it was an investment by the club, and I didn't feel guilt – not even when the other players were playing well and I was playing badly.

Clubs continued to sniff around, and it seemed only a matter of time before the St Mirren board would buckle. Tony Fitzpatrick and I were invited to have our picture taken standing beside £500,000 in cash, our reported joint valuation, which added a little more pressure. Aberdeen, whom Fergie was now managing, and Celtic were said to be interested in me, but Willie Todd was adamant that he was not going to sell me to another Premier League club.

Things got ugly between me and Clunie, and he left me out of the side for a while during the winter. It was the best thing that could have happened to me. It gave me a rest, and when I came back I had my best spell at the club. I'd enjoyed my enforced holiday, but I realised that if I got back to playing, I had a better chance of getting a move. I returned in the New Year, and I was back in the groove quickly, my form earning me a call-up to Jock Stein's Scotland squad for a game against Belgium.

In February, I notched in a 1–0 win over Motherwell at Love Street then followed it up with a goal at Morton in a 2–2 draw. The following month, I scored a hat-trick in a 3–0 away win at Motherwell, who were managed by Ally MacLeod. I'm not sure if he felt he had made a mistake by not taking me to Argentina, but I enjoyed it anyway and would have scored about six if it hadn't been for their keeper Stuart Rennie.

A week later, we beat Morton 3–1 at Love Street on my birthday, and I scored again. However, what I remember most about that game was Andy Ritchie's goal for them. It was one of the best that I have ever seen. Andy had no mobility, but he was a great striker of the ball. That said, I still don't know how he did what he did that day. Straight from a corner, he curled a ball, which gathered pace as it came into the penalty box, right over Iain Munro's head as he stood on the line guarding the post. It was magic, even for Andy. I was not doing too badly myself. My goal in the 3–2 defeat against Hibs was my eighth in five games.

While I was playing for a transfer, the Premier League title race between Celtic and Rangers was coming to the boil, and I found myself at the centre of a curious incident on 21 April 1979 when I scored after 24 minutes to give us the lead at Parkhead. When play restarted, Celtic defender Andy Lynch said to me, 'What are you doing scoring against us? We're going for the league.' I looked for a smile or a smirk, but he was deadly serious. I replied, 'Sorry, Andy. You're a defender. You're supposed to stop me.' He knew I was a Celtic fan, but what was he expecting? Did he think I was going to let them win the game so they could carry on with their title challenge? St Mirren were paying my wages, and I had to give them 100 per cent. The Old Firm fans knew I would try my hardest against their sides, and I had the goal statistics to prove it. He had no right to say that to me, and I was very disappointed. In the end, Celtic came back to win 2–1 and went on to win the league with a dramatic 4–2 win over Rangers.

Lynch's comment upset and unsettled me for days afterwards, but the following Saturday I had an exceptional game against Aberdeen at Pittodrie with, as it turned out, the Liverpool scouts watching me. I didn't score, but we won 2–1 through goals by Bobby Torrance and Billy Stark after Steve Archibald had scored the opener. I scored in a 1–1 draw with Partick Thistle at Love Street, which turned out to be my last goal for the club before I was sold. I ended up top scorer at the club again with 13 league goals, and I was proud of that.

When Jim Clunie called me and asked me to come to Love Street as soon as possible, I knew something big was happening. I had ruled out the possibility of going abroad, but I had no idea where I wanted to play my football. Unfortunately, I had no one to talk to about the move.

When I got to the ground, Clunie said, 'Liverpool want to sign you. They want us to travel down to Preston to meet them and sign today.' I was obviously aware that big clubs were interested in me, but when a concrete offer was actually made I was stunned. I hadn't been aware that Liverpool were serious contenders. Aston Villa, Arsenal and Ajax had seemed to be the front runners. Liverpool were one of the greatest clubs in Europe. They had won the European Cup in 1977 and 1978, and there was a Scottish presence at Anfield in the shape of Graeme Souness and Alan Hansen, while Kenny Dalglish had signed the season before for a record fee of £440,000. It seemed like a perfect move for me. St Mirren had decided to cash in – whether I wanted to go or not. Jim told me that chairman Willie Todd had said to him, 'We will give Frank £20,000 to sign for Liverpool,' so I felt like a pools winner even before we set off for Lancashire.

As Jim and I began our journey to England, we started talking about wages, and I was saying, 'Well, I'm on £150 basic with St Mirren, so I will ask Liverpool for £300 and a £10,000 signing-on fee.' By the time we drove past Motherwell, it was, 'I wouldn't mind getting £350.' When we crossed the border and passed Carlisle, I was up to £500, and when we arrived at the hotel in Preston I wanted £600 per week and a £40,000 signing-on fee. Who knows what it would have been had I been going to sign for Portsmouth?

Liverpool chairman John Smith and chief executive Peter Robinson, two wonderful men, were waiting for us. I was wondering how the negotiations would pan out. Would we be there for hours? Would I have to stay overnight at the hotel? We sat down and Peter Robinson said, 'We are giving you £425 per week. You will get a £12,500 signing-on fee. Sign there.' I took his pen and signed. It was the quickest transfer deal ever made in football. I looked to Jim for some sort of inspiration, a sign that it was a good deal or that I should have asked for more, but he was just nodding inanely. He didn't have a clue, either.

St Mirren got the cheque the next day. They had bought me for a couple of hundred quid from Kilsyth and had sold me for £270,000, big money at the time and not a bad profit, you would think. But it obviously wasn't enough. I asked Willie Todd for my £20,000 and got nothing. He fobbed me off, and I had no comeback. I should have got that promise down in writing, but I had no business sense. I needed an agent. Clubs didn't want agents then, and no wonder; they could do anything they wanted with guys like me.

The £20,000 was the equivalent of a house, and although I wasn't too bothered at the time I soon had cause to curse Todd. My first wage was £425 plus a lump sum of around £4,000, one of three payments of my signing-on fee – my net was £842. Income tax was at 83 per cent that year, and nobody told me about it. I owed about £900 in lawyers' fees for moving and buying a house in Formby. Only I could have ended up out of pocket after getting a big-money move from St Mirren to Liverpool.

5

THE LEAVING OF LIVERPOOL

I had been scoring and making goals at St Mirren in a team that was struggling in the Premier Division. I had big clubs like Arsenal and Ajax after me as well as English giants Liverpool – arguably the greatest club in Europe at the time – but I didn't get a cap until I moved from Love Street. Sound familiar?

Jock Stein had taken over from Ally MacLeod after the carnage of the 1978 World Cup in Argentina. Bob Paisley, the Liverpool manager, and Jock were very good friends, and that might have had something to do with my elevation in status. I had been in and around a few squads, had been named in the provisional 40-strong World Cup squad (but had missed the cut) and I had played for the Under-21s, but I didn't expect to be brought into the Scotland squad for that summer's Home International Championship. Nevertheless, I was determined to grab my chance when it did come along.

As a kid, I had dreamed of playing for my country. I was as much a Scotland fan as a Celtic fan. There is a notion that Scottish Catholics, especially those from the west of Scotland, have an affinity to Ireland, but I have always felt 100 per cent Scottish. Even though McGarvey probably sounds like a typically Irish name – Rangers fans certainly thought so – the McGarveys were a very proud Scottish Catholic family. We would all sit in front of the television to watch matches against England – often the only ones shown live – and we would all be up out of our seats every time Scotland even came close to scoring.

In fact, there was no Irish influence in our house. None of my grandparents were Irish, but even if one of them had been, or there had been any other link, I would never have contemplated playing for Ireland before Scotland. Of course, I was well aware of the connection between Ireland and Celtic, and that was never a problem with me when I was growing up as a Celtic fan or when I played for the club. I have visited Ireland on many occasions, and I have always been made very welcome, but I have never hankered to be an Irishman. A lot was made of the talented Celtic midfielder Aiden McGeady choosing the Republic of Ireland over Scotland at a very early age, but that was down to him, and I respect his decision – but it wouldn't have been mine.

Indeed, my patriotism doesn't end in the sporting arena. I have found myself becoming increasingly nationalistic over the years. Like most parents of working-class families in Easterhouse, Mum and Dad were totally supportive of the Labour Party, but those well-established loyalties have, for various reasons, grown weaker in Scotland. I am a fan of Alex Salmond and a supporter of the Scottish National Party, and I always vote for them. Like a growing number of people, I would like to see Scotland become independent. We have the resources, the infrastructure, the education and legal systems, and the character and personality to be a successful nation in our own right. After independence, we then can vote along party lines and decide for ourselves which shade of government to embrace, but first of all we have to break free from the union.

So, with all my burning patriotism, imagine how disappointed I felt when my first appearance for Scotland was as a last-minute substitute who didn't get a touch of the ball. I had been left out of the 3–0 defeat by Wales in Cardiff on Saturday, 19 May 1979 but had been put on the bench for the game against Northern Ireland at Hampden the following Tuesday night, which was only a fortnight or so after I had joined Liverpool.

My new Anfield teammate Kenny Dalglish, captain on his 62nd appearance, was playing in attack with Joe Jordan. Everton goalkeeper George Wood made his debut, and George Burley and John Wark, my teammates at Under-21 level, were both earning their second caps. Northern Ireland, managed by Danny Blanchflower, had Pat Jennings in goal and Pat Rice, Allan Hunter, Jimmy Nicholl, Sammy McIlroy and Gerry Armstrong playing, but, in reality, the tournament was dying a slow death.

There were just over 28,000 people inside the rickety old-style stadium to see Arthur Graham score the winner in the 76th minute, and there were far fewer when I replaced him with a minute to go. Instead of bursting with pride, as I thought I would be if I were ever to get the chance to play for Scotland, I felt embarrassed. I made a couple of runs before Welsh referee Clive Thomas blew for full-time. I sneaked off the pitch, hoping that most people hadn't noticed me. However, in the dressing-room afterwards, Dalglish, in his own caustic way, asked me if I had touched the ball, knowing fine well the answer. Some of the other guys laughed, and I thought to myself, 'Thanks, Jock.'

There was some financial consolation, though. The new boot contract I had signed after joining Liverpool stated that each time I played for Scotland I would be paid £125. So, I earned £125 for one minute's work, an hourly rate that made me easily the highest-earning footballer in Britain. I would have given that money and a whole lot more to have been picked to play against England at Wembley the following Saturday. Like most Scots, Wembley was as much of a Mecca as Hampden, and I had dreamed of becoming a hero against the 'Auld Enemy'. But I obviously hadn't shown enough in the 60 seconds at Hampden against Northern Ireland and was left out of the 3–1 defeat, which ended the home internationals for another year.

But there was still another international game to be played before we broke up for the close-season, and it was a glamour friendly against World Cup holders Argentina at Hampden on 2 June 1979. By the time the star-studded visitors flew into Glasgow, I hadn't played competitive football – my Hampden minute aside – for about six weeks. My general fitness wasn't bad, but I had lost my edge.

It was a beautiful summer's day, with nearly 62,000 fans turning up to get their first sight of some of the players who had beaten Holland in the World Cup final 12 months earlier. Alberto Tarantini, Daniel Passarella, René Houseman and Jacinto Luque were in the visitors' side, but they were all overshadowed by a diminutive teenage midfielder going by the name of Diego Armando. It's safe to say that the crowd left Hampden that day talking about Maradona rather than McGarvey, even though I played quite well.

Maradona was simply out of this world, scoring the third goal in a comfortable 3–1 win. In a match that was at times an exhibition of Argentine brilliance, Luque had put the visitors two goals ahead, and they were cruising to the final whistle when Arthur Graham scored a consolation for us.

Former Scotland boss Tommy Docherty had sung the praises of the stocky little midfielder in the press before the game and said that he would have spent £10 million on him – Dalglish, remember, cost £440,000 – so I thought, 'This guy must be good,' even though I didn't know him from Adam. Maradona didn't let the Doc down. He was better than a £10-million player. He was strong and pacy, and his movement was superb. His close control was sublime, and his awareness and vision were a joy to watch, even as an opponent. He remains the greatest player I have ever seen or played against.

I have a feeling that Maradona won't remember me. I played alongside Kenny that day, which was a great pleasure and a privilege. He also had great vision, and he helped me through the game. I had a few half-chances to score, but I wasn't sharp enough, mentally or physically. One of my shots hit the shoulder of the keeper and flew over, and when I was in a decent position inside the Argentina penalty area I tried to cut the ball back when I should have opted to go for goal myself. These little bits of luck or misjudgement can make all the difference to a striker's game, but I'm certain I would have scored if I had been match fit. I felt that it was like another trial match for me, and I needed to be at my peak of fitness. I can't say that Jock didn't give me my chance, but I thought that it was a bit unfair that I got my first caps when I was trying to settle in at another club and hadn't played much football. Why wasn't I given a chance when I was playing out of my skin for St Mirren?

Disappointment, my overwhelming feeling as I walked out of Hampden following the Argentina game, is a word that best sums up my Scotland career. You need a run of games at international level to get to grips with the different styles of play, and even that doesn't guarantee success. Although it may be heresy to say it, Dalglish was a much more potent player for Liverpool than he was for Scotland. He knew how everyone at Liverpool played, and they knew how Kenny played. But at Scotland he was continually paired with different strike partners and with different midfielders, and it was more difficult for him to replicate his Liverpool form for his country.

During the summer of 1979, as I rested before resuming pre-season training with my new club, I didn't have time to dwell too much on my international frustrations. I had the small matter of trying to break into one of the greatest club sides in Europe. The Tuesday after signing for Liverpool, Pauline and I sat in the main stand and watched them beat Aston Villa 3–0 to win the First Division title for the third time in four years. It was an incredible night as I watched a packed Kop, holding around 20,000 people – more than St Mirren got at Love Street – go through their full repertoire. The Scottish contingent of Souness, Hansen and Dalglish were playing, and I was even afforded some recognition by the supporters when they interrupted their backing for the team to sing my name. It felt fantastic, and I sheepishly gave them a wave.

Liverpool fans love their football, and they love their Scots. Billy Liddell became a legend after his exploits in the 1940s and '50s. And Bill Shankly had almost single-handedly reinvented the club in the early '60s with players such as Ian St John and Ron Yeats.

When the final whistle went, my first thought was, 'What a great place to play your football.' My second thought was, 'How the hell am I going to get into that team?'

As it turned out, my fears were well founded. I couldn't have gone to Liverpool at a worse time. They had a system at Anfield that had stood them in good stead for years. They continually built a good second team to keep a great first team on their toes. That was the single most important reason why they were so successful. Liverpool's game was based on good players passing the ball. The second team was set up to play like the first team: patient enough to wait for their chance to exploit a weakness or an opposition player out of position. They also worked hard before signing a player, making sure that he had the right character for the club. I had spoken to John Smith and Peter Robinson in 1977 after Liverpool had come to Love Street for a game to commemorate our centenary year. I had a great game that night, and they wanted to see what kind of personality I had.

It was undoubtedly a magnificent system for Liverpool – but it wasn't magnificent for me. I had been kidding myself on. I had been bought as a second-team player. I was there to keep the pressure on the first-team players, like a theatre understudy. That I had cost £270,000 meant nothing to manager Bob Paisley. Defender Avi Cohen was signed for a fee of £200,000 from Israeli side Maccabi Tel Aviv, and he went into the reserve team beside me.

And what a reserve team we had, with Steve Ogrizovic, Colin Irwin, Alan Harper, Ronnie Whelan, Kevin Sheedy, Avi Cohen, Sammy Lee, David Fairclough and Howard Gayle all playing regularly, supplemented from time to time by Steve Heighway and Dave Watson. Every one of those players eventually got a chance in the first team – except me. Most of them went on to become very successful players either at Liverpool or elsewhere.

Strangely, Bob Paisley insisted that I change in the first-team dressing-room before I was a first-team player, and I thought that was wrong. I would have rather gone into the second-team dressing-room with the players I was playing alongside every week. To be honest, I felt a bit overawed. This was one of the best dressing-rooms in the game. Dalglish, Souness and Hansen were good to me, as were Terry McDermott and most of the other players, but ultimately I wasn't a first-team player. There weren't cliques as such, but they had their own groups, and most of them were older and more experienced than me. I had gone from being a big fish in a small pond to a very small fish in an enormous pond, and that hit my confidence.

Life away from football provided its own distractions, and

Pauline and I found it difficult to settle on Merseyside. We bought a three-bedroom detached house in Formby, a desirable area, for £22,500, and we were able to put a £12,000 deposit down. We spent most of our time decorating the house before our first son Paul was born in August. I wanted him to be Scottish, so Pauline travelled back to Scotland for the birth. I received a phone call when she was almost ready and drove to the hospital in Paisley to be with her when our first child came into the world. I was ecstatic but also an emotional wreck after seeing what Pauline had gone through. Bob was old-fashioned in many ways and didn't believe that the birth of a child was an excuse for a player to miss training, so I was up at the crack of dawn the next day to drive back to Liverpool, Pauline following me about a week later. It wasn't ideal for either of us, but we were determined to make the move work.

Despite a strong Scottish presence at the club, the player with whom I got on best was 'Crazy Horse' Emlyn Hughes, the Englishman whom the Scots loved to hate. Even some of his own teammates from north of the border didn't see eye to eye with him, and, within the confines of the Anfield dressing-room, Kenny would occasionally have a go at him. However, I thought Emlyn was a terrific guy – even for an Englishman.

The only player I didn't take to was England defender Phil Neal. He was the only one who didn't make me feel welcome at the club. Our initial spat happened in the most childish of circumstances. I was sitting in the bath after training, and he came in and said, 'That's my bit of soap you're using.' I was equally petty and replied, 'I don't see your name on it.' He then started to shout at me, trying to bring me down in front of the other players. Being a new boy, I wasn't sure how to react, but I didn't forget it.

Surprisingly, pre-season training at Liverpool was easy. Given the success the club was enjoying at the time, I had presumed that it was built on a pre-season of physical torture.

But I cruised through the close-season and was raring to go at the start of the new campaign. I scored twice for the second team when we played the first team in a bounce game, so I knew that I hadn't lost my nose for a goal.

When it became clear that I would not be put straight into the first team, I aimed to do my best for the reserves. It would surely be only a matter of time before Bob came calling for my services. I started the season well in the Central League with David Fairclough as my strike partner and Howard Gayle on the wing. I scored in my second game, against Sheffield United, and again a fortnight later at home to West Bromwich, and I then hit a hat-trick at Leeds the following week. The reserve team was brilliant, but I wanted out of it as soon as possible.

With Kenny an instant hero on the Kop, my only other way into the first team was past David Johnson, who just happened to pick that season to hit his best-ever tally in a red shirt. It was demoralising to jump on the bus after a reserve game and hear on the radio, 'Another David Johnson goal gives Liverpool victory.' After a while, I started thinking, 'Christ, do these guys never get beat?' Mostly not was the answer. The first team scored a record number of goals and won the league by a record number of points, and they hardly picked up an injury, certainly not among their attackers. It was unbelievable, and it was sending me round the bend.

Terry McDermott and Graeme Souness were among several Liverpool stars who implored me not to get impatient, telling me that some players spent two years in the second team before they got their chance. But, if anything, that just made matters worse. I couldn't bear to contemplate two seasons in the Central League. I could have been playing regular first-team football at almost any other club in Britain. Therefore, appearing in front of 500 to 1,000 people every week was not what I wanted to be doing.

While my football career had stalled, my gambling career

sped into overdrive. For the first time, my penchant for the bookie's had begun to affect my life. Despite the overeager tax man, I was earning more than I had been in Scotland, and I even bought a brand-new car. On the face of it, we had all the traditional trappings of success. But in addition to having more spare cash, I also had more spare time, a very dangerous combination for anyone with any sort of addiction.

I was finishing training at about 1 p.m. and going straight to the local bookie's. Before long, I was comfortably spending three hours a day in there, longer than I was spending at the Melwood training ground. You have no friends in a bookie's; you tend not to want to speak to anyone, preferring to be cocooned in your own little world of favourites, odds and accumulators. I was zombie-like, staring at the newspapers, looking for some divine inspiration that seldom came.

Most of the success I did have was as a result of tips from Emlyn, the only guy in football who was owed money by the bookies. He was friendly with some of the top jockeys, and he would come into the dressing-room in the morning and tell all the players which horses he thought would win that afternoon. One day, he told us about a horse that he thought was a certainty, saying that it was the best tip he had given us in weeks. I only put £10 on at a time at that point, but I made an exception that day. I put on £30, and the horse won at 6–1. I was well chuffed with that. Emlyn had put on £100. The thing was, he walked out of the bookie's to go home and count his money, and I stayed and gave them their money back. I wasn't gambling to win money. That was the sad thing about it. It was just a fix for me.

I couldn't tell Pauline about my problem, and I don't think that she was affected too much. I was home at 5 p.m. every night – only because that was when the bookies' closed for the day – and despite my gambling we had a good life.

I needed more money, so I chapped on Bob Paisley's door

one day and told him that I thought I had been playing well. I then asked for a £50 per week rise. Without taking a moment to consider my request, he said, 'No problem. It will be in your wages at the end of the week.' I thought, 'Damn, I should have asked for more.'

As I turned to leave, he said, 'By the way, I was speaking to trainer Frankie Durr this morning, and he said that two of his horses would win this afternoon.' He then told me, in his quietly spoken manner, that he had been speaking to Michael, who also had a horse out that day that had a good chance of winning. I thought, 'Surely he can't mean Michael Stout, the legendary trainer at Newmarket?' I couldn't believe I was getting this kind of information. The meeting was getting better and better. He went on to tell me that Henry Cecil had also told him that he had a good horse running that afternoon. I thanked Bob and walked out of the door armed with four of the best tips in the land and a £50 rise. I put £10 on each of them, as I normally did. I didn't have the bottle to put them all on an accumulator. Needless to say, they all won, and instead of being happy with the hundreds I had won I was unhappy at losing the thousands that an accumulator would have provided.

I was getting caught up in the madness of gambling. After getting those tips from Paisley, I found myself thinking, 'I'm a professional footballer, and I could also become a professional gambler.' I was in a dream world, failing to take into account all the other days when I was leaving the bookie's without a penny in my pocket. My losses were slowly creeping up on me. I opened a bank statement that showed I was taking out £50 from the bank every day and losing it. Half my wages and more were going to the bookies every week.

My football ambitions were temporarily put on hold. Although I was playing well and scoring for the reserve team, I wasn't as fit as I could have been. I was very ambitious, and I thought I had the potential to be a great player. I could create, and I could finish, but I needed to be stronger. Before I moved to Liverpool, I pledged to go back to training in the afternoon and use all the facilities available to make me a better player. But when the afternoon came, the bookmakers won over extra training, not by a short head but by a distance. So, it was a double whammy. I had less money than I should have had, and I wasn't fulfilling my potential.

One day, I was introduced to a Liverpool supporter, a really nice guy, who just happened to be my bank manager. I thought to myself, 'Thank you very much. This could be to my advantage.' I was paying my mortgage and bills, but for the first time in my life I was in a wee bit of debt. I arranged to go in and see him and told him that I wanted a loan to build an extension to my house. He looked at the title deeds and said, 'Frank, you've got three bedrooms and only one child. Why do you need an extension?' I told him that we had people visiting us from Glasgow all the time, and I wanted the extra space. I told him that I needed around £3,000 to cover all the costs, and he said, 'It'll be in your bank account in the morning, no problem.' I checked my account the next day, and I had £3,000 extra in it. I thought, 'Wow, that was easy.'

The loan was gone in a month or two. A few months later, my friend the bank manager came round to the house and asked where the extension had been built. I looked him straight in the eye and told him that the building firm I had employed to do the job had taken my money up front and done a runner.

Lying was becoming easier. When you are a compulsive gambler, you also become a liar and a cheat. And for the first time in my life, gambling had really begun to mess with my head. I was frightened of what was happening to me. I was out of control. Pauline was still unaware of what gambling was doing to me. I was coming home in the evening and switching back to the role of husband and father. But I was telling her lies, saying that I was at training every afternoon, and I hated myself for that. What kind of man does that? The non-gambling Frank was a brilliant guy; the gambling Frank was a horrible guy. I was two people in one, and the question was: which Frank was going to win?

The bad guy was winning at that time. I was disgusted with myself that I had spent the bank loan and had nothing to show for it. I catalogued all the things I could have done with the money I'd lost over the years, and I felt worse. I had dreams of going into property, using my joinery skills to convert houses into flats, but the gambling was taking that away. It was taking everything away. By the end of the season, I tried to sell my new car to fund my gambling, such was my desperation.

Despite my personal turmoil, I continued scoring goals for the reserves. However, a little bit of ambition was being knocked out of me with each passing week. Liverpool were the best team in Europe, and I was part of it, but I felt that if I had scored 100 goals in the reserves, I still wouldn't have got into the Liverpool first team.

Despite my frustrations, I was pleased to make an appearance at the club's famous Christmas party. It was traditional for the new boys to sing a song at the night out – or at least that's what I was told. Unaided by musical backing, Avi Cohen stood up and surprised the whole Liverpool squad when he revealed a more than decent voice. I surprised them again – but only with my dreadful rendition of Rod Stewart's 'Sailing'. There was mild amusement and some boos as I droned through the first verse, but when I carried on into the second verse my teammates decided that throwing the remnants of their dinners was the best way to show their feelings. I carried on regardless, louder and more out of tune, and they all rolled about laughing. However, for the most part, laughter was in short supply.

I thought my chance had come in March 1980 when I was

drafted into the squad for the game against Ipswich at Anfield. At that time, there was only one substitute, so it was a straight fight between me and David Fairclough, a tall, gangly, ginger-haired player who was to become the original 'Super Sub'. He wasn't a great player to play alongside, and despite him having been called up during the season on several occasions my good form in the reserves at that time led me to believe that Bob Paisley was going to give me the nod. It was another wrong call. After Bob's team talk, he ran through the team, finishing with, 'Dalglish and Fairclough up front. McGarvey on the bench.'

The Liverpool team that day was Ray Clemence, Phil Neal, Alan Kennedy, Phil Thompson, Ray Kennedy, Alan Hansen, Kenny Dalglish, Jimmy Case, David Fairclough, Terry McDermott and Graeme Souness, a line-up that is difficult to argue with, but it didn't make me feel any better. I was raging, and I could hardly share the general enthusiasm when Fairclough gave us the lead after only eight minutes. Ipswich, who had George Burley, John Wark, Alan Brazil and Terry Butcher playing for them, equalised through Eric Gates, and as I got changed after the game I knew it was all over for me.

Bob Paisley hadn't done anything wrong. He was getting hassle from all the other players in the second team, all of whom were first-team material, but he could only play 11 at a time. Nevertheless, I was in no mood to be logical. I went in and asked for a transfer. He told me to take it easy and that he would give me six or seven games when I was ready. But I thought that I was ready. He could see that I was determined to leave, and he said that although he didn't want me to go he wouldn't keep anyone who wasn't happy. I entered his office at 10 a.m. and was back in Glasgow by 2 p.m. I phoned Pauline and told her I had asked for a transfer and that we would probably be going back to Scotland. She left the decision up to me. Wherever I would have gone, she would have followed.

I decided that I was going to start a new life with either Celtic or Aberdeen, both of whom I knew were keen on me. I would make a few bob with my signing-on fee and clear off my debts. Fergie and John Clark, Billy McNeill's assistant at Celtic, had both been phoning me for months. Fergie would ask my advice on certain players whom he was interested in buying, and he was forever telling Pauline that Aberdeen was a lovely place to live . . .

Fergie called me and arranged to meet me at 5 p.m. in an Italian restaurant in Glasgow. He offered me £275 a week, as much as anyone was on at Pittodrie, although a good bit less than I was earning at Liverpool. He also offered me a £20,000 signing-on fee and a two-year contract. In addition, he said that if we had not won anything in that time, he would let me go on a free transfer. I don't know how he managed to persuade the Aberdeen board to agree with that clause – if, indeed, he ever told them about it – but that's how confident he was of winning trophies at Pittodrie.

My head said that I should go to Aberdeen. I thought they had a better squad than Celtic, including a good defence, a good goalkeeper and a brilliant midfield, and if they could get someone to put the ball in the net, they would be an excellent team. Fergie had great faith in me. He would have helped me to improve as a player, and Frank the non-gambler wanted to become better at his trade. Frank the gambler knew that Fergie would have stopped him gambling. He knew that I had a problem, and if he had been forced to put a bodyguard on me to stop me gambling, he would have done that.

Jock Wallace phoned me and asked to me join him at Leicester City, who were in the English Second Division at the time. He told me that he had wanted to sign me for Rangers but had not been allowed to, which confirmed Willie

Thornton's part in getting me to St Mirren. But after being at Liverpool, regardless of whether or not I played, I didn't want to go to Leicester.

In the end, I followed my heart. I wasn't destined to play for Liverpool; I was destined to play for Celtic. All my dreams were at Parkhead. I wanted to score the winner against Rangers at Celtic Park with two minutes to go and net the winner in a Scottish Cup final. I met up with Billy McNeill and Celtic chairman Desmond White and was offered a four-year contract worth £300 per week. The fee was to be £270,000, the same amount I had cost Liverpool. I said, 'OK, I'll sign.'

I phoned Fergie to tell him my decision, and he was unhappy to say the least. He claimed that I had betrayed him. He said that I had agreed to sign for Aberdeen, but I hadn't made any promises. However, Fergie informed me in his own inimitable way that we were finished.

6

···

PARADISE FOUND

As the steel studs gradually came through the soles of my boots on the red ash of Celtic's infamous Barrowfield training ground on my first day with the club, I thought, 'Have I made the biggest mistake of my life in coming here?' I hadn't considered training facilities or anything like that when I'd discovered that Celtic wanted to sign me. However, I was soon made aware of the contrast in the way players at Liverpool and Celtic were treated at their respective clubs. Liverpool had their own training ground with at least three pitches, a gym, a big bath and everything you could ask for, and we would get the bus there from Anfield each morning and back again in the afternoon. When I asked about transport to training at Celtic, I was told, in no uncertain terms, to run along London Road.

I'd decided to wear studs on my first day because it was raining, but when I got to Barrowfield I discovered that we were training on a red-ash pitch. I said to the other players, 'Is this it?' Celtic had been in existence for 92 years at that time, and, make no mistake, they had made a fortune from football, yet here I was, their record signing, training on red ash along with the rest of the club's assets. We had no gym or indoor hall, so we had nowhere to train our upper bodies. Weeks later, a group of players were doing sit-ups in the foyer of Celtic Park when Desmond White and some businessmen visiting the stadium passed through and had to step over us. It was an absolute disgrace. The mentality was that the Lisbon Lions had trained there and had won the European Cup, so why should we have it any better?

The money saved by not building a training ground certainly didn't go towards the players' wages at Parkhead, circa 1980. Irene McDonald, the club secretary, and a guy called 'Flax' would go to the bank every week to pick up £7,500 for the wages. Two games against Rangers would pay the wages for a year. There were few improvements made to the stadium, so the money must have gone somewhere. The players used to speak about it, but we couldn't work out where the money was going.

People often ask me why I just didn't sit in the Liverpool reserves for the duration of my contract and take the money, but there was no financial advantage in doing that. Good money could only be made from signing-on fees and bonuses for winning trophies. Our basic wage, although better than the average working man, wasn't ridiculous. Besides that, I was an ambitious footballer who wanted to show people what I could do.

Agents were a thing of the future, and the clubs took full advantage of their playing staff. You could be forced out of the game by a club if you didn't play ball. I should have asked for more money and a bigger signing-on fee, because I had more than one team after me, including two clubs fighting for the Scottish Premier League title. A good agent would have played the clubs off against one another, the way they do now. But my desire to play for Celtic was well known to the club, so it weakened my bargaining power.

I wanted £300 a week basic to sign for Celtic, and they gave me that, so I was happy enough, even though it was a significant drop from what I was on at Liverpool. The better-paid players at Parkhead, such as Danny McGrain, Roy Aitken and Davie Provan, were on £150 a week basic, and the Rangers players were on the same. I had been getting that as a basic wage at St Mirren two years previously.

But money wasn't the be-all and end-all for me. Perhaps it should have been, given the way I was spending it. My signing-on fee cleared my debts, but I wasn't freed from the clutches of gambling on returning to Glasgow. We stayed in the McDonald Hotel in the south side of Glasgow while we looked for a house. I had my eye on a big property in Pollokshields that cost about £48,000, a fortune at the time. The profit from the sale of the house in Formby plus my signing-on fee meant that I had enough money to buy it, but it would have left me stretched, and I wanted to save some money for gambling – how sad is that? – so we didn't purchase it. We settled for a place in King's Park, still on the south side of Glasgow, near to Hampden Park. I had money to gamble, and at the time that was more important to me than my long-term future.

Choosing Celtic over Aberdeen, however, seemed less of a gamble, despite my admiration for the Pittodrie club. When I arrived at Parkhead, Billy McNeill's side were ahead of Aberdeen in the title race and had just beaten Spanish giants Real Madrid 2–0 in the first leg of their European Cup quarter-final tie. I was brought in at a crucial point of the season to boost a squad that included Peter Latchford, Alan Sneddon, Danny McGrain, Murdo MacLeod, Roy Aitken, Roddy McDonald,

Tom McAdam, Tommy Burns, Vic Davidson, Jim Casey and Mike Conroy. I was fighting for a place in attack with George McCluskey, Davie Provan and Johnny Doyle, and it tickled me that Bobby Lennox, one of the Lisbon Lions, was still playing. Bobby was a wonderful player, and even in his mid-30s he was still a great trainer and full of enthusiasm.

I got chatting to Tommy Burns in the dressing-room one day, and we compared backgrounds. I knew that he was about the same age as me and had come from Glasgow. I asked him which school team he had played for, and when he said St Mary's it came back to me. I said, 'Ah, you were the guy with the red hair.' Tommy asked me who I had played for, and I told him St Clare's but that he might remember me from my nickname. He said, 'So, you were Stiney. I remember you.' Tommy then quickly let the other players know my nickname, which saved them the bother of making one up. It was an extremely sad day for me when he passed away in May 2008 after losing his battle with cancer. My thoughts were with his wife Rosemary and their four children, as well as with my four children, who had all loved Tommy.

I had no time to acclimatise at Celtic. I signed on Monday, 10 March 1980, and I played against St Mirren on the Wednesday. We drew 2–2 after leading by two goals, Doug Somner, my replacement at Love Street, scoring twice after George McCluskey and Johnny Doyle had given us the lead. It was as uneventful a debut as you would fear making. I wasn't fit, but Celtic wanted me to play to put another 5,000 on the attendance, which was important at that time. Celtic's average home gate that season was under 30,000, although, of course, you had to take some of those official attendances with a pinch of salt.

Celtic Park was a different place to the 60,000-capacity, all-seated, covered arena that modern-day fans attend. The main stand was the only seated area, and the small terraced area known as the 'Jungle' across from it housed the diehard Celtic fans. Apart from a few thousand season-ticket holders, most games were pay at the gate and attendances varied. Rangers and Aberdeen games were invariably played out in front of full houses, and in time matches against Dundee United also attracted big crowds.

These days, Celtic and Rangers are guaranteed large attendances for all home games because of the season-ticket culture, which, from a business point of view, is fantastic. What business doesn't want its customers to pay for a full year's worth of goods up front with no possibility of a refund? Form counts for almost nothing. Fans are all but obliged to attend the home games after paying in advance, and when they are at the stadium they also buy other stuff, such as food, drinks and programmes.

The refurbished Celtic Park is magnificent, but I am glad that I played in front of the Celtic crowd of my day, because the Jungle was an intense place. If it was a big game at Parkhead, Celtic fans would be up for it, and the Jungle helped create a terrific atmosphere that would inspire the home players and intimidate the away side. If an opposition player went to take a throw-in in front of the Jungle, especially a Rangers player, he would get pelters from the Celtic fans.

However, after my first few games for the Hoops, I was worried that I would soon be getting pelters from the Celtic fans. I cursed the pre-season training at Liverpool. Even though I had only been away ten months, the Scottish game seemed quicker, and I found it hard to adjust. I had suffered from cramp against St Mirren on my debut, which didn't augur well for the run-in.

I turned out against Kilmarnock three days later, hoping to get off the mark, but drew a blank again in a 1–1 draw. It was too early to panic, but only just. The punters care little about how fit and sharp players are. They presume that if they are on the pitch, they should be at their best. They also presume that if their record signing is a striker, he should score goals. When I read in the press forwards saying that it doesn't matter who scores the goals as long their teams win, I think, 'Rubbish.' The only thing strikers really care about is their goal tally.

I lost my first-team place temporarily when Celtic flew to Madrid to try and defend their 2–0 lead at the Bernabéu. I wasn't eligible to play, but at the behest of Billy I went along to lend moral support to the rest of the lads. I was very disappointed with the stadium after all I had heard about it. It was just a big concrete bowl, and even though there were 110,000 fans there that night there was a better atmosphere at Celtic Park on a European night.

But Real Madrid were a formidable side in front of their own fans. George McCluskey and Johnny Doyle had scored at Parkhead, but even with a lead it was always going to be a tough task to get through against a team that included English wide-man Laurie Cunningham, German sweeper Uli Stielike and Juanito.

Not for the first time, a Scottish club would rue missing an early chance in Europe. We started the game well and looked like we could cause a shock, but after just ten minutes, with Madrid all over the place, George shot past the post with only their keeper Mariano García Remón to beat, and that was our chance gone. Madrid scored just before half-time, which gave them the boost they needed, and it was no real surprise when they got the other two goals they needed in the second half. I would have to wait another year for my European debut.

Overcoming Real Madrid had perhaps been fanciful, but we certainly fancied our chances of a Premier League and Scottish Cup double. My own aims were a little lower. I was looking for a goal, and I was the most relieved man in

Glasgow when I scored my first for the club against Hibs in a 4–0 win at Parkhead at the end of March. We struggled in the first half, and I was worried that it was going to be another day to forget, but when Bobby Lennox scored with a penalty just after the break we relaxed and started to play. I scored next, a close-range header from a brilliant Davie Provan cross – the first of many I would get from him – and it was good to get off the mark. Johnny Doyle and Roddy McDonald made the scoreline look a lot healthier, and I came off feeling satisfied with my contribution for the first time since my arrival.

I wasn't daft. I had been struggling, and John Clark wasn't about to let me think that nobody at Celtic had noticed that I wasn't living up to my fee. He would walk around Celtic Park whispering, 'The ink on that contract is not dry yet, Frank.' Neil Mochan, one of the backroom staff who had been a great centre-forward for Celtic, used to laugh at John, which would encourage him further. Neil had his own motivational methods. When you had missed a sitter, he would say in a jocular manner, 'You're no good. You'll be out of here soon.' Despite it all being light-hearted, I knew that there was a serious element to what they were saying. I would see it in the years to come at Parkhead when players would come and go after failing to live up to expectations.

Despite my goal against Hibs, I sensed that the fans were uncertain about their big-money buy from Liverpool. However, one sure-fire way to silence doubters and get the Celtic faithful onside is to score the winner in an Old Firm derby, which is exactly what I did on Wednesday, 2 April at Parkhead. I had scored against Rangers for St Mirren, but my first Old Firm goal, as clichéd as it might sound, fulfilled a boyhood ambition, and it remains a special memory.

It was the biggest crowd I had played in front of, and I could hardly hear myself think in the opening moments of the game. Like most Old Firm matches I played in, it was a tough battle, with little football played, and I was growing increasingly exasperated as the game continued goalless. I wasn't playing well, but I just wanted half a chance; I was confident that I could take advantage of anything that came my way. It looked like a point was all we were going to get out of the game until Roy Aitken chased the ball inside the Rangers penalty area at the Celtic end of the ground with just two minutes to go. The ball looked as though it was going out, but Roy was not a player to give up on lost causes. He stopped it on the line, turned and quickly crossed. For the first time in the game, I was unmarked, and I gratefully headed the ball past Peter McCloy from about ten yards out.

The place went crazy, the noise nothing like I had ever heard before. Off I ran to the Jungle, demonstrating a turn of pace that I had yet to show during games, to celebrate in front of the fans, soon joined by my teammates. I had scored a late winner against Rangers at Celtic Park – it was a dream come true.

I was so pleased in the dressing-room after the game. My first day of training at Celtic had made me doubt my decision to move to the club, but I knew then that I had made the right choice. Aside from bragging rights in Glasgow, we had given ourselves a massive confidence boost. But we still couldn't dismiss the challenge of Aberdeen, especially with Alex Ferguson as their manager.

Most football people in Scotland were sceptical about the staying power of the Dons and, for that matter, Dundee United, despite growing evidence that they were capable of challenging the Old Firm's dominance. Aberdeen had won the League Cup in 1976–77 and lost in the final to Rangers two years later. Earlier in the season, they had beaten Celtic in the League Cup quarter-final only to lose in the final to Dundee United after a replay, the first major trophy the

Tannadice side had won. The two clubs were on the brink of becoming labelled the 'New Firm', but Scottish football fans had not witnessed a genuine threat to the Old Firm since the early 1960s, so the scepticism was not too surprising.

However, I knew Fergie better than most. I had witnessed his desire and his managerial abilities, and I knew his team would provide a powerful challenge to the two Glasgow giants. But as I basked in the glory of my Old Firm winner, I didn't think it would come so soon. Three days after our win over Rangers, we welcomed Aberdeen to Celtic Park, knowing that victory would all but seal the title. Our confidence could hardly have been greater. We had taken three points from four in our previous two encounters against them, and Billy said in his programme notes, 'Victory against Aberdeen would assuredly place the Premier League championship within our grasp.'

But we lost our unbeaten home record with a 2–1 defeat and the season subsequently began to unravel at an alarming rate. Johnny Doyle scored midway through the first half to equalise Drew Jarvie's opener, but we never really got going, and Aberdeen came back in the second half and scored the winner through Mark McGhee. Worse was to follow. The following Tuesday, we suffered a 3–0 hammering at Dundee United thanks to a second-half double from Davie Dodds and a John Holt strike. From the high of an Old Firm victory, we were now hanging onto the title won so famously the previous season when Celtic had beaten Rangers 4–2 at Parkhead with ten men.

A 5–0 Scottish Cup semi-final win over Hibs at Hampden allowed me to reacquaint myself with George Best, who was by then performing at Easter Road. He remained peerless in terms of skill, but he had lost another yard since our Anglo-Scottish Cup encounter. The 2–0 home win over Kilmarnock in our next match looked to have put us firmly back on track, but it preceded Celtic's worst defeat of the season. When Roy

Aitken gave us the lead after seven minutes against Dundee, there seemed no danger of us losing five goals to a less than average Dens Park side – but we did. The wheels had come right off our title challenge, and it seemed like we were powerless to do anything about it. Billy was quoted in the papers afterwards as saying that it was the most humiliating result of his career, and the players felt little better.

My arrival at Celtic should have been the boost that would propel us to the title, but the reality was that the team had run out of steam. It was a disastrous end to the season. We were a much better team than Dundee and should never have lost 5–1 to them, but in my opinion we weren't that good a team. Billy had won the title the season before, but he was still building, and there were clearly problems that needed to be addressed. Another home defeat by Aberdeen in a rearranged fixture the following Wednesday, this time 3–1, gave Fergie's side the advantage. They had the momentum of coming from behind, and we could do nothing to stop them.

While we were drawing 0–0 with St Mirren on the last day of our league season, Aberdeen were romping to a 5–0 win at Easter Road. Technically, they had to be beaten 10–0 by Partick Thistle in the last game of the season in order for us to have a chance of catching them, but that was obviously never going to happen. Television pictures recorded Fergie bouncing around the pitch after the game against Hibs, celebrating with his players, not giving a toss about one of his protégés who had snubbed him to go to Celtic. I was again left wondering if I had make the right decision. We finished one point behind Aberdeen and five ahead of St Mirren, who were followed by Dundee United and Rangers, our old rivals finishing halfway down a ten-team league.

The Scottish Cup final against Rangers at Hampden presented us with our last chance of silverware that season. A cup-final victory always sends the fans away for the summer on a high and can temper the disappointment of an indifferent league campaign. That's what we were hoping, anyway. We had enjoyed a relatively easy cup run that season, beating Raith Rovers 2–1 at Celtic Park in the third round and then overcoming St Mirren 3–2 after extra time in a replay. We beat Morton 2–0 at Parkhead in the quarter-finals and Hibs in the semi-final at Hampden.

The 1980 Scottish Cup final didn't produce the greatest Old Firm encounter ever seen at Hampden, but it did produce the most notorious sporting event ever to take place in the 'Dear Green Place'. A post-match riot between the two sets of supporters that resulted in an alcohol ban in Scottish football stadiums overshadowed an easily forgettable game.

I wasn't in the best shape going into the match and wasn't performing to the best of my ability. I had only scored a couple of goals since I had arrived from Merseyside, and John Clark's mantra – 'The ink's still not dry, Frank' – had begun to annoy me. What I needed was a rest and a good pre-season, but that would have to wait.

A packed Hampden was bathed in sunshine that day, but it failed to inspire the players. I had three or four chances, and I should have taken at least one of them, but after ninety minutes neither side had scored, so the game went into extra time, the last thing anybody wanted. The first team to score was the most likely to win, and luckily enough it was us. We were shooting towards the Rangers end when Danny McGrain found himself with the ball coming at him at the edge of the box. He sclaffed his shot, but George McCluskey stuck out his heel and redirected it past Peter McCloy. It wasn't the greatest cup-winning goal, but it was enough for us to win the trophy.

There have been various explanations as to how and why

supporters from both clubs found themselves chasing each other up, down and around Hampden, but at the time the players didn't even know it was happening. Someone in the dressing-room said, 'There's people fighting on the park,' but we didn't take it in. We were just relieved that we had won something that season after the disappointment of losing out on the title. As we left Hampden ready to celebrate long into the night, we knew a cup win over Rangers would make for an easier summer for us all. It was the next day before we realised the magnitude and scale of what had happened between the two sets of fans.

I invited everyone back to my house for a party later that night. I had a bar in my house, and it had always been a focal point for family and friends when they visited. During a boisterous evening, I heard a knock on the door. I opened it to find Kenny Dalglish, Bobby Murdoch and Jimmy Johnstone standing there, all with carry-outs. Kenny, of course, was a former teammate at Liverpool, and we had played together for Scotland, but, nevertheless, three of my heroes, three of the greatest Celtic players ever, wanted to come into my house. Eight years earlier, I had been a wee boy kicking a ball around in Easterhouse. Now, three Celtic legends were at my door asking if there was any chance of joining my party! I said to them, with a deadpan expression, 'Who are you guys? Can I help you?' I enjoyed that moment. And it was a great party, because as well as winning a trophy the players knew that they would get a good bonus. It meant that all the players and wives were a bit more merry than usual.

I awoke the next day, expecting to see the papers full of pictures of us celebrating our Hampden win, but instead they concentrated on the riot. Pictures of fighting fans and a policewoman on horseback trying to restore order were everywhere. It was like the game itself had not taken place.

The fallout was dramatic. Alcohol was quickly banned from football grounds in Scotland, which was a radical step to take, given that the terracing carry-out had been part and parcel of football for as long as anyone could remember. It was felt that drunkenness had contributed to the trouble in and around Hampden, so banning it was the easiest way to deal with the problem. How to eradicate the bigotry associated with the Old Firm was a more difficult proposition. Rangers, with their no-Catholic policy, bore the brunt of the criticism.

The *Sunday Mail* carried out a survey among Catholic footballers, asking if they would be willing to be the first to break the decades-old practice of no Catholic players playing for the Ibrox club. Former Leeds and Scotland skipper Billy Bremner wanted 'no part' of the discussion, Leeds winger Arthur Graham, who later played for Manchester United, was more vehement, saying, 'Not for a king's ransom,' while my old St Mirren teammate Tony Fitzpatrick, Leeds defender Frank Gray and Dundee United centre-half Paul Hegarty claimed that they wouldn't have a problem with signing for Rangers. I was quoted as saying that I would have 'no compunction' about joining Rangers, which was pretty brave of me, if I may say so, given that I was the only one asked who was actually playing for Celtic at the time. Funnily enough, I don't remember getting any stick from the Celtic fans for saying it.

I would have loved to play for someone like Jock Wallace – he was my kind of man. He had tried to sign me for Rangers and Leicester City, so I knew that he had a lot of respect for me, as I had for him. I understood when former Rangers player Alfie Conn said that he wanted to sign for Jock Stein when he came back from Tottenham in the mid-1970s. Good managers can make you want to play for them, and Wallace, in my mind, was a good manager. However, I am more or less certain that the Rangers fans would not have welcomed me to Ibrox with open arms, because I was something of a hate figure for them at that time. I know that my name alone was enough to set most of them against me. Rangers fans would sing 'Frank McGarvey's wife's a whore' to try and put me off, but it was inspirational, because I knew that they were worried about me. I would have been more annoyed if they hadn't sung anything about me.

The only time I felt a bit scared among Rangers fans was when Davie Provan and I were trying to get into town after I had scored the winner in a 2–1 win at Parkhead. We used to go a circular route past Shawfield and through the Gorbals, but we were in a rush so drove down London Road and through Bridgeton Cross, only to run into a big crowd of Rangers fans milling around. I put my head down so that they wouldn't see me, but they noticed Davie, and they started shaking the car. Mounted police who were making their way back from the game cleared a path so we could get away.

Although sectarian chanting and name-calling was as prevalent among Old Firm fans in the 1970s and '80s as it is now, I never had a problem with Rangers players during games, apart from the time that Davie Cooper called me a Fenian bastard. Rangers players, and players in other teams, called me everything under the sun to try and upset me, but no one ever mentioned anything to me, directly or indirectly, about my religion. Therefore, I was disappointed with Davie taking it that step further, even though I knew that it was said in the heat of the moment. We had come through the ranks together, he at Clydebank and me at St Mirren, so I was taken aback when I realised what he had called me, and I replied, 'Davie, it's me you are talking to. What's all this Fenian bastard stuff?' I think he realised that he had spoken out of turn.

Nearly 30 years on from the riot at Hampden, things have changed at Ibrox, and for the better. Rangers have since signed Catholics, and both Rangers and Celtic have come up with a series of educational initiatives to ease the tensions between the two clubs. However, there is still a problem with bigotry at Ibrox and Celtic Park, and it is going to take a long time before it becomes a thing of the past. The disease is not confined to football, or to the Old Firm, but it is mostly found in the west of Scotland and is most publicly expressed through the support of Celtic and Rangers. When sectarianism is eradicated for good, it will be a great day for this country.

7

· ·

MY FINEST MOMENT

The 1980 cup-final win over Rangers had cushioned the blow of us losing our league title to Aberdeen. The fact that we hadn't surrendered the championship to Rangers also made our lives a little easier that summer. Meanwhile, Scottish football was in something of a flux. It was trying to come to terms with a non-Old Firm club winning the league. It hadn't happened since Kilmarnock had snatched the title on the last day of the 1964–65 season, and no one was sure what to make of it. With Dundee United winning the League Cup, a new football landscape was emerging. Celtic would have to look further afield than Ibrox for potential challengers in the season ahead.

At the start of the 1980–81 campaign, there wasn't anyone at Celtic Park more determined than me to win back the title. As well as finding my top form and proving to the Celtic board and supporters that I was worth the money that had been laid out for me, I wanted to prove to Fergie that I had made the right choice by opting for Parkhead. But he had struck the first blow. He had won the title without me, and that bugged me all summer.

I had enjoyed a good rest and was raring to go when I reported back to Parkhead, but my initial enthusiasm soon dissipated. Pre-season training was much harder than at Liverpool, and in particular the runs around Strathclyde Park were torture. Long-distance running wasn't my idea of fun, especially after six or seven weeks off. Most of the players struggled, except John Weir, one of the young guys in the squad. He didn't really make an impact on the first team at Parkhead, but when it came to fitness he was in a league of his own, and we used to watch him disappear into the distance as we panted behind.

After a pre-season tour of Germany, I was bursting to start my first full season at Parkhead. Billy had basically the same group of players at his disposal, although a young Irish goalkeeper called Packie Bonner had replaced Peter Latchford, and we had an even younger addition to the squad: an 18-year-old striker by the name of Charlie Nicholas, who had been pushing at the door the previous season.

It wasn't a bad debut season in Scotland's top-flight for Charlie – he would be named Scotland's Young Player of the Year at the end of the campaign – but I was just as pleased with my own efforts. I would end up being the country's top scorer with 23 league goals to start a run of Celtic players winning the award. George McCluskey followed me with 21 the following season, Charlie came next in 1982–83 with 29 and Brian McClair netted 23 the year after. It was indicative of the way we tried to play football.

Billy was proving to be a very good manager. We weren't overburdened by tactics or bogged down by instruction. It was uncomplicated football. Defenders cleared their lines, midfielders were expected to help their defence and provide for the strikers, and the strikers . . . well, the strikers were there to score goals. If you didn't produce the goods, you were out of the team. We played 4–3–3 with Davie Provan, for the most part, wide on the right. That season Billy would pick two strikers from Charlie, George and me. When I was playing, I was left mostly to my own devices, and I certainly wasn't asked to track back and defend, although I worked defenders hard when they were in possession.

I was aware that I hadn't pulled up any trees since I had arrived from Liverpool. And despite a decent pre-season, I didn't start the campaign in good form, which was a worry. I found that the pool of goodwill engendered by my winner in the Old Firm game was in danger of running dry. At Celtic, the pressure is on to do the business all the time, so when I went just two games without scoring at the start of the season people were asking questions. The media, without coming straight out and saying it, were trying to make me out to be washed up.

After I scored a double against Kilmarnock in a 3–0 win at Rugby Park on 16 August, which was a huge relief, Bobby Maitland wrote in the *Daily Express*:

> The icing on the cake was the return to form of big-money buy Frank McGarvey. Since returning from Liverpool, Frank has taken time to settle, hardly surprising after the upheaval of the last 12 months. The manner in which the slick striker took his goals suggests that there are a lot more to come in the season ahead.

It was a polite way of saying that I had been crap until that game.

The injury I picked up against Killie allowed Charlie Nicholas to make his debut as a substitute, and he showed glimpses of what the Celtic fans could expect from him during the following two seasons. But I was fit enough to score a hat-trick against Hungarian side Diósgyőri Miskolc in the first leg of the preliminary round of the European Cup-Winners' Cup at Parkhead. Strangely enough, all the goals in a 6–0 win came in the second half. George McCluskey got two and Dom Sullivan scored the other, and it could easily have been double figures. After the game, the same reporters who had questioned my ability were asking me how many I would score by the end of the season: 20, 30, 40? One headline the next day screamed 'Celtic's Mr Goals'. I thought, 'Make your minds up, guys!'

The prospect of another Old Firm game at home the following Saturday promised more glory, but not for the first time in that fixture things didn't go as planned. When Tommy Burns gave us the lead, we looked to be on easy street, and even when Jim Bett equalised I thought we were still the more likely side to take the points. You could have picked your own odds if you had wanted to put a few bob on Rangers left-back Alex Miller scoring the winner. To be fair to him, it was an unbelievable goal. There were only a few minutes remaining when he received a throw-in from Willie Johnston and hammered a shot past big Packie from 30 yards. I stood at the other end of the pitch and wondered where that strike had come from. It was the first goal that I could remember him scoring, and it was the only time I remember Rangers beating us at Parkhead in my time at Celtic.

It was Alex who signed me for St Mirren when I left Celtic five years later. We were chatting one day, and I said to him, 'That winner you scored for Rangers at Celtic Park with a couple of minutes to go must have been one of the best goals you ever scored?' When he replied, in all seriousness, 'Och, I've scored better goals than that,' I nearly fell off my chair.

I rarely heard Billy complaining about referees, although he had a go at Eddie Pringle after Miller scored the winner against us. Once again, the accusation of Celtic paranoia raised its head, and it's an issue that still surrounds the club. Celtic have always had a hate–hate relationship with officials, and there are few Celtic fans who do not buy into the theory that there has been an orchestrated conspiracy against the club for decades, if not since the day it was formed in 1888. But I am not one of them. I have no cause to believe officials in Scottish football are anything other than honest.

I have been a Celtic fan all my life. I played professional football for over 20 years and was also a manager, and I believe that refereeing decisions even themselves out. When I played for Celtic, referees made bad decisions and good decisions. I would go down in the box, and it was a stonewall penalty, but nothing was given. At other times, I would hardly be touched, and the referee would point to the spot. But I think officials are genuinely fair. No referee ever scored a goal or decided who won the league. It is always the best team that wins the league.

However, that is not to say that officials aren't affected by big crowds. If I'm a referee and there are 50,000 Celtic or Rangers fans screaming for a penalty that is a 50–50 decision, or bringing to my attention an incident that I might have missed, then it is only human nature that I will be pressured into giving a favourable decision. It's the same all over the world: big teams such as Manchester United, Real Madrid and Bayern Munich seem to get the occasional decision in their favour. I think it really is that simple. Due to the high number of televised games and cameras that are trained on football nowadays, contentious decisions are highlighted more than they have ever been. But even the pundits in television studios sometimes cannot agree after watching the same incident four or five times, so what chance do referees have with one look at an incident in real time? Referees have been an integral part of the game since the beginning. Is it not about time we left them alone?

The one referee I would have gladly strangled, however, was a Greek. He was the exception who proved the rule. We won through to the first-round proper of the European Cup-Winners' Cup with a 7–2 aggregate victory against Diósgyőri, where we met Politehnica of Romania. Charlie scored a double at Parkhead in the first leg, but we lost a goal and travelled with only a 2–1 lead. Almost from the first whistle, I sensed that it was going to be a long night. Roddy McDonald's sending-off was a joke, but I wasn't laughing when I was next. I was dismissed after the referee refused to award us a stonewall penalty when I was right through on goal and ready to score. A Romanian defender brought me down, and I couldn't believe it when the referee waved play on. I ran over to him shouting, and he sent me off for dissent. Our 1–0 defeat meant that we went out on the away-goals rule.

At a function after the game, I noticed that the Greek ref was with two beautiful blonde girls, and I gave him the wanker sign. He ended up coming over to our table and pushing me. Billy came to my aid and someone attacked him. There was a stramash, and Billy ended up under a table, even though he'd just been trying to help me. In the end, I was suspended for two games. Nowadays, it would have been blown up into an international incident, but it was quickly forgotten, like our European hopes for yet another season.

The next time we played Kilmarnock, Charlie and I grabbed a double each in a 4–1 win at Parkhead, but again it was followed by a defeat by Rangers, this time 3–0 at Ibrox. They had just been knocked out of the Anglo-Scottish Cup by Chesterfield the previous Wednesday, one of the worst embarrassments in their history, so we had been more than confident going into the match, but once again it showed how difficult it was, and still is, to predict Old Firm games.

On 8 November, we lost 2–0 at home to Aberdeen, a game memorable for a Celtic fan coming onto the pitch from the

Jungle and attacking Gordon Strachan. If Joe Harper and Derek Johnstone had been the pick of the bunch when I was at St Mirren, then wee Gordon was the top player in Scottish football when I returned. But he infuriated the Celtic fans, and the supporter certainly came on aiming to cause him harm. Gordon had a lucky escape, thanks to the intervention of a couple of Celtic players.

I was scoring my share of goals, but we were blowing hot and cold, and when we lost 4–1 away to Aberdeen on 28 December it looked like Fergie was going to get one over on me again. They demolished us that day, and immediately after the game the bookies made them 4–5 favourites to keep their title, while we were 7–4 to win it back. Rangers were 8–1, which showed that they weren't at the races yet again.

For some reason, it all fell into place for us after the turn of the year. On New Year's Day, I scored another two against Kilmarnock, in a 2–1 win at Rugby Park. I then scored two against Morton in a 3–0 home win and another along with Charlie in a 2–1 win over Dundee United at Parkhead. When I scored one in a 3–0 win over Hearts at Tynecastle on 31 January, it was our fourth Premier League win on the trot, and Aberdeen losing 1–0 to Rangers at Ibrox did us a big favour. We were back on track.

Scottish Cup wins over Berwick Rangers and Stirling Albion, the latter a 3–0 win in which I scored, kept our hopes of retaining the trophy alive. The bandwagon was gathering pace. Charlie Nicholas scored two in a 3–1 win over Rangers at Parkhead to cement his newfound hero status with the Celtic fans. It was our first league win over Rangers that season, and we were on our way to taking the title back from Aberdeen.

I always enjoyed playing against Rangers. When I played for St Mirren, I loved coming up against guys such as John Greig, Tom Forsyth and Colin Jackson, and none of them would mess about. If you were going into a fight on a Saturday night, you would want those guys with you, but on a football pitch I was quicker than them. I knew it and they knew it, and they did their best to curtail my advantage. Defenders were allowed to come right through the back of you in those days. As long as the defender got a touch on the ball – and even at times when he was nowhere near it – it wasn't a foul. If a defender could take the ball then come straight through you, that was all the better.

Intimidation was part of the game. You would hear the centre-halves saying to their partners loud enough for you to hear, 'Just go through him right away, and he won't want to know.' You were bracing yourself in the first few minutes when the tackles were for free, as they say. Fergie taught me to use my elbows, which I did on occasion. I would also hold onto the centre-half and then shove him away from me when the pass was on its way. That would give me a couple of yards of space, and I could then try to turn with the ball. Tom Forsyth didn't like me elbowing him in the ribs, but, then again, I didn't like him booting me and the ball into the air. I actually thought that Forsyth was the easiest Rangers defender to play against, while it was always very difficult to get any change from John McClelland. He was good in the air, very strong, a good tackler, quick and he could read a game.

But McClelland was a rare example of finesse at Ibrox in the early 1980s. Rangers signed a lot of players who would kick their granny, and Gregor Stevens was just another in a long line. Like his former teammates at Motherwell, McVie, McLaren and Millar, he seemed to be just as interested in bodies as the ball.

I had also fared well against Celtic defenders when I was at Love Street. When Jock Stein was coming to the end of his time at the club, he didn't sign the best of players. In fact, Celtic were a poor team with some ordinary players, such as Joe Filippi, John Dowie and Frank Munro. Big Frank was the slowest player I had ever come up against. I couldn't believe that he was Celtic's centre-half. He was extremely unfit, and in one game I cruised past him at half-speed after giving him a five-yard start.

Celtic had the least intimidating centre-half in Scotland during my time at Parkhead in Tam McAdam. He is probably the most mild-mannered defender ever to have played football. He would never intentionally hurt anybody, and if he did, he would apologise. He was originally a centre-forward and a good finisher, and, as with Derek Johnstone, I could never understand why he wanted to play at the back. In particular, Tam seemed out of place in the madness of an Old Firm game, in which everybody seemed to lose the plot at one stage or another. I took a battering from Rangers defenders, but ironically the only time I ever got involved in any form of retribution was with one of their midfielders, Alex MacDonald.

A small, wiry midfielder, Alex was a great footballer, whom Rangers could always depend on, but he definitely had a nasty streak, although, to be fair, he took it as well as giving it out. Alex liked to come in over the ball sometimes, and I didn't like that part of his game, especially when I was the victim. On one occasion, he did me down at the Celtic end at Parkhead, and I was raging. Revenge was the only thing on my mind as I chased after him when Rangers were on the counter-attack. As I got up beside him, I quickly checked to see that the referee and then the linesman weren't looking and elbowed him as hard as I could. He fell to the ground, and there was a big cheer from the Jungle. I regretted it immediately. The fans started chanting, 'There's only one Frank McGarvey,' which was the only time I didn't want them to sing my praises. It was one of hundreds of similar incidents that took place up and down the country that went unpunished, mainly due to the lack of cameras at games. But it was wrong, nonetheless.

I had scored eight goals in the first nine games of 1981, so my confidence was up and my ego was being satisfied, but I was still taken aback on 14 March 1981 when I experienced my greatest moment in football. Most people assume my finest moment was my cup-winning goal against Dundee United in 1985, and it is probably the thing most people – not just Celtic fans – remember about my career. In fact, my best moment came in a Premier League win over St Mirren at Parkhead. It wasn't the third goal of a hat-trick in the 7–0 win that I cherish most; it was the reception I was given by the Celtic fans after I scored my second right on half-time that will live with me for ever.

Roy Aitken headed us into the lead after 12 minutes, and when I grabbed the second in 37 minutes the points were safe and our title challenge was still on course. Just before half-time, I picked up a Mark Reid pass, beat three St Mirren players, getting up off my knees to go past one of them, and crashed a 30-yarder into Billy Thomson's top right-hand corner. A loud roar went up. I ran to the Jungle to take the acclaim, and the players all congratulated me. I walked back to the halfway line and the crowd were still roaring. At that moment, the half-time whistle sounded, and the fans were still cheering. I walked up the tunnel to a standing ovation from the punters in the main stand. The Celtic fans are probably the hardest supporters to please in world football, so I was overwhelmed by their reaction. I had never heard that type of acclaim for a Celtic player before.

My stomach started to do summersaults on my way to the dressing-room, and I made for the toilet. One of Billy McNeill's tactics was to give a player a bit of stick when they were playing well in order to keep them focused. When he turned round to say, 'And as for you, Frank,' all he heard was me throwing up. I emerged to a great roar of laughter from all of the other players. The dressing-room was buzzing, and we duly went out and scored another four goals to make it 7–0.

I got my third after the interval to secure the match ball,

and a goal by Charlie Nicholas and a late double by George McCluskey completed the rout, making us the bookies' favourites to win the league. The *Sunday Post* reporter ended his match report by naming me the Man of the Match and writing, 'If Frank McGarvey has played a better game than this, it was in his dreams.' He was right, and I still get goose bumps when I see that second goal on tape.

Despite my form, I was still out of the international scene. Scotland played about eight games that season. I should have been in the team, never mind the squad, but Jock Stein wouldn't pick me. He had selected me to play against the world champions Argentina when I was between clubs and not match fit, but when I was in the form of my life he ignored me. I thought that was unfair. I began to wonder if he left me out because I had snubbed his old pal Bob Paisley at Liverpool. I had to say all the right things in the press every time a squad was announced and my name was omitted, but it was niggling away at me.

Any notions of us winning the Double were gone when we were knocked out of the Scottish Cup in the semis by Dundee United at Hampden after a goalless draw in the first game. As usual, everyone thought that the provincial side had blown their chance, but United were magnificent in the replay. However, Jim McLean's Hampden hoodoo was taking shape, and they lost to Rangers in the final after another goalless first game.

But we were well on the way to the title. Charlie Nicholas scored against Rangers in a 1–0 win at Ibrox, and we were all but champions. We had done to Aberdeen what they did to us the year before. They thought they had won the title at Christmas, but we came from behind to win it, clinching it with a 3–2 victory at Tannadice. We finished up on fifty-six points with Aberdeen seven adrift. I was the top scorer in Scotland with 29 goals in total, and I had my first Premier Division medal. My decision to choose Celtic over Aberdeen had been vindicated.

8

MY NAME IS FRANK, AND I AM A COMPULSIVE GAMBLER

Aside from my international frustrations, with a Premier League winner's medal in my pocket and the accolade of being Scotland's top scorer, I should have had little to worry about as I looked forward to the 1981–82 season. But almost without me noticing, my gambling pilot light had turned into a healthy blaze. My marriage was still strong, and I was delighted with the birth of our second son, Sean, on 5 February 1981. Having two young kids around the house should have added to my sense of responsibility, but I just couldn't control my gambling.

I had slipped into the same sort of daily routine that had characterised my time at St Mirren and Liverpool. After training, Davie Provan, Roy Aitken and I used to go to Joe's

Kitchen on London Road and feed our faces full of sausage, egg and all the crap of the day. There wasn't a bowl of pasta to be seen. Then I would come home, drop off my car and walk round to the bookie's that sat beside The 100 Acres pub. I was in there every weekday, leaving only when it closed or when I had run out of money – usually the latter. I thought I was an expert, but I was a typical mug punter. I didn't have a clue about the horses that were running, but I was betting on every race, and when you do that you have no chance of winning. Bookies only need a dozen customers like me, and they can't go wrong.

I got a tip at the beginning of the season for a horse that was running the following February. It was 66–1 at the time, but I held off until the day of the race then put a few quid on at 10–1. When it won with a bit to spare, I was kicking myself that I hadn't lumped on when I was first tipped off. So, even when I was winning, I was still unhappy.

I didn't get the 'big win' that gamblers like to recall in justification of years of losses. You hear stories of ordinary punters getting accumulators up which win them ten grand or high rollers putting twenty grand on a horse and it winning at 20–1, but I never experienced anything like that. My biggest win was around £2,000. My brother Joseph loaned me £25 one day when I was skint. I put three fivers and a £10 treble on, and all the horses 'stoated', as they say. The last horse was priced at 12–1, and that was the one that made me most of the money. It won by half a length, and the adrenalin rush was unbelievable. I gave Joseph his money back and more. But I didn't want to win money to do something positive with it. I just wanted to gamble to win money to gamble again.

There wasn't a gambling culture at Celtic as such, but, as at every club and in every workplace, there were a few folk who liked a punt. So, when I wasn't betting on horse racing at the bookie's, I was playing cards on the team bus and in team hotels. The card schools usually consisted of Davie Provan, Roy Aitken, Mike Conroy, Tam McAdam and me, and we would play pontoon from the minute we boarded until we got off – and remember, we travelled a lot. We would all have our lucky days. Sometimes I would win, and sometimes I would lose, but there was never a huge amount of money on the table.

Pre-season trips always provided plenty of opportunity to get a card school set up, and as there was often more money involved it would get that little bit more serious, as it did when we convened in a hotel room in Seattle to play pontoon. The dealer, who usually has the best chance of winning, was allowed three rounds before passing the cards onto the next guy. However, the dealership could change hands at any time if the kitty was successfully 'shot'. Shooting the kitty meant you would gamble against the money the dealer had accumulated during his time as dealer. For instance, if he had £50 in the kitty after one round, it would cost you £50 to try and shoot him. It was a high-risk move that could cost dearly if you messed up.

It was my third round as dealer, and as a few of the boys had tried to shoot me and had lost, I had about £180 in the kitty, a considerable sum of money at that time. As I dealt the last hand, I noticed excitement in the Paul McStay corner, and I assumed he had been given an ace. As expected, he wanted to shoot me, but I reminded him that he only had £80, and the rules were that you could only bet what you had on you – borrowing was not allowed.

However, Paul wanted to borrow the money from Willie McStay, his brother, who was in the room but not playing, claiming it should be allowed because he was family. I let him know that rules were rules and were not to be broken – especially when I was in danger of losing £180. We had a vote on it, and it went 5–4 in Paul's favour, some players refusing to notice that since he was the only one with a brother in the team he could use his unfair advantage over them at a later stage. We then discovered that Willie didn't have enough money to cover the kitty. It was a farce. There was another vote to see if Willie could borrow from someone else to give the necessary funds to Paul, and again the McStay camp won the vote 5–4. There hadn't been a hand played in 20 minutes. I was angry, because I knew that £180 was enough to keep me going for the rest of the tour, and I could see it disappearing.

I gave Paul his second card, and it was a ten. His camp were all jumping about on the beds, shouting and singing to wind me up. I needed 21 to win the money, the dealer getting the advantage if both hands are equal. When I turned an ace over, the McStay celebrations came to a halt. The tension was wonderful. My heart was pounding, but I was milking the moment. I still didn't believe I could win, but I wanted to prolong Paul and his supporters' agony. It took me two minutes before I turned over the next card, which happened to be a ten. It was one of those sweet moments in life.

It was my turn to celebrate. The McStay camp were shattered, especially Paul and Willie, who had not only failed to win the kitty, but had to pay back the money they had borrowed. 'Cool Hand' Frank was £360 better off. I tucked the money in my pocket and told everyone that I was exhausted and had to go for a nap. Two or three of them voiced their displeasure as I slipped out the door, but I laughed all the way down the corridor and back to my room. It showed how quickly a fun game of cards could escalate into serious gambling, but it didn't have any effect on team spirit, although I did take a dim view, in the nicest possible way, of those players who had voted against me.

We were bullish about our prospects of retaining our title the following season, but once again the European draw was unkind, and we exited the European Cup in the first round to Juventus. I watched the first leg at Celtic Park from the stand as I served my suspension, and it was an education. Liam

Me at St Clare's Primary School

Starting out at St Mirren

At St Mirren during the 1976–77 season. Back row: Robert Torrance, Phil McAveety; front row: Billy Stark, Tony Fitzpatrick, Fergie, me, Bobby Reid

Me (top right) in a Liverpool pre-season team picture, 1979–80

Playing for Scotland against Argentina (© Getty Images)

Taking on Aberdeen's Willie Miller, the best defender
I ever played against (© SNS Group)

Playing for Celtic against Rangers (© Getty Images)

Celebrating with Davie Provan after winning the
1985 Scottish Cup final (© Getty Images)

Pauline and me after the 198
Scottish Cup final (© *The Su*

Winning the Scottish Cup with
St Mirren during my second spell
with the club (© SNS Group)

LEFT TO RIGHT:
Pauline, Paul, Sean, me,
Jennifer and Scott at
Scott's communion

Winning the Man of the
Match award after playing for
Clyde against Queens Park in a
Skol Cup match in 1992

Jennifer and me in Los Angeles at the Celtic Supporters Club in 2001

Jennifer and me on a
Caribbean cruise in 2003

Me with my mum, dad and granddaughter Chloe

With my family (left to right): Scott's wife Sarah, Scott,
Jennifer, me, Sean, Paul's wife Carla and Paul

Me back on the tools (© *The Sun*)

Brady, who would subsequently become Celtic manager, was pulling the strings for the classy Italian club, and we were more than grateful when Murdo MacLeod scored to give us a 1–0 win to take over to Turin for the second leg.

As I warmed up before the game in Italy, a firecracker exploded right beside me, and I jumped up in the air in fright. When I realised what had happened, I pretended that the leap was part of my exercise, just like the guy who trips walking for a bus then breaks into a run to mask his embarrassment. So, for a few minutes I jumped about the pitch with my teammates looking at me as though I was daft. God knows what the crowd were thinking.

Forsyth, Stevens and McVie were tough on the legs, but Juventus defender Claudio Gentile was another notch up altogether. He was easily the dirtiest player I had ever played against. Apart from crunching me any time he could, he spat on me and pulled the hairs out of the back of my legs. I had never spat on anyone in my life before, but I became so enraged that I went up to him during the game and gobbed on him. He knew it was coming and moved his head out of the way. Despite being underhand, Gentile wasn't the best defender I had faced, and I got the better of him that night, but it was to no avail. Juventus scored twice, and we were out. Not for the first time, an Italian team did just enough to get through. I went looking for Gentile after the game. I wanted to give him a right-hander as a cheerio present, but he was nowhere to be seen, which was probably lucky – for me.

It was another disappointing European campaign, but there was a bigger blow to the club waiting around the corner. On 19 October, Johnny Doyle was electrocuted whilst rewiring the loft of his home in Kilmarnock. He was only 30 at the time of his death, and we could hardly take it in. Johnny was a diehard Celtic supporter. He didn't have a crucifix taped to his chest during games, as one myth goes, but he was the only player that would turn up for matches wearing a Celtic scarf with his suit.

But it would be hypocritical of me to say that Johnny and I were best pals. The truth is we didn't get on. In fact, Johnny was Davie Provan's best mate at the club, which I couldn't understand, because Davie had been brought from Kilmarnock to take his position.

Doyley was very aggressive and easy to wind up, and some of the players, including me and Vic Davidson, picked up on that. He was once sent off the training field by Billy McNeill after threatening to give Charlie Nicholas a doing for continually nutmegging him. He always had to have the last word, and I can still recall him shouting back at Billy as he sloped off down the road.

Johnny would walk around Celtic Park saying to the players, 'I'm the man.' I would wind him up by replying, 'You're not the man. I'm the man. How can you be the man when you're in the reserves?' He didn't like that.

However, he wasn't really one to trifle with, as I found to my cost during the pre-season tour of Germany in 1981. We were hanging around the hotel waiting for the bus to arrive to take us to our next destination. It was scheduled to come at 1 p.m. In front of the other players, I pointed to Johnny and said, 'If you are not out of this room at two o'clock, I will be coming to sort you out,' and walked away. I was giving myself plenty of latitude, but, of course, the damned bus was late. I asked Billy when it was coming, and he replied, 'About five past two,' something I didn't want to hear.

All the players and management staff were in the hotel foyer at 2 p.m., and I came along the wooden corridor stamping my feet so that they would hear me. I walked over to the players and shouted, 'Anybody seen Doyley?' I heard a voice at the back saying, 'I'm here. What about it?' I couldn't back down. I had to go through with the pantomime. I said, 'You were told to be out here for two o'clock. Why are you still here?' He wasn't playing along and, in complete seriousness, growled back, 'What are you going to do about it?'

I walked over and tried to pull him up, and we started wrestling. I was pretending, but he wasn't, and as we rolled around I could feel his anger. He managed to get my head in a stranglehold, and if he had turned it a little bit more, he would have snapped my neck. For a second, that's what I thought he was trying to do. I grabbed a part of his anatomy that made him release me immediately, and the arrival of the bus thankfully ended our spat. That incident was typical of Doyley. He was a permanently coiled spring.

There was the occasional set-to at training, which kept the dressing-room in gossip. On one occasion, Davie Provan and I had a bust-up behind the goal at the Rangers end at Celtic Park. He swung a punch at me and nicked me. I then tried to get at him, and the players jumped in to split us up. Billy sent the two of us to the dressing-room, walking us in to make sure that it didn't go any further. We didn't speak for a few days, but we were pals again soon enough. I heard Charlie Nicholas saying to Davie on the radio a couple of years ago, 'Do you remember that time when you got a hold of Frank?' but he was talking a lot of rubbish. Charlie was trying to exaggerate the story, but there was nothing to it.

It would be wrong to overstate the occasional tensions that surface at every football club. The Celtic dressing-room was not a place for the faint-hearted, but it was a fun environment most of the time, and there were lots of big characters at the club, such as Tommy Burns, Davie Provan, Roy Aitken and Graeme Sinclair. We all got on well and enjoyed each other's company, and two or three of us would attend every supporters' function. As we saw it, meeting the fans was an extension of our jobs. The fans loved it, and because of that contact there was a greater connection between the supporters and players than there is at the club now. I don't know why, but over the years players have been allowed to lapse from their duties towards the fans, and it's not just the foreign players who are not interested.

The only time I questioned my responsibilities was when Davie Provan and I were invited to a supporters' function in Belfast at the time of the hunger strikes. I have nothing against the good people of Ireland, but Belfast at that time was not the best place to be for a Celtic player. The atmosphere in the country was incredibly tense. Three very well-connected locals, to use a euphemism, met us at Belfast Airport and drove us to the Europa Hotel, which is referred to as being the most bombed hotel in Europe. The whole city seemed full of hatred. A soldier pointed a gun to my head when the car we were travelling in was stopped at a security check. After the third round of security checks to get into the hotel, I was thinking, 'Where is the fun in this?'

Davie recalls that the hall in which the function was held had pictures of the hunger strikers on the walls, but, to be honest, I only remember my Irish karaoke number. Davie and I were encouraged to give the punters an appropriate song for the occasion, but Davie didn't know any, and the only one I knew was 'Merry Ploughboy', which I had learned at school, so it was up to me. I sang the first verse – the only one I really knew – and the fans rescued me by joining in. In truth, I was never so glad to get out of a place in all my life.

On another occasion, the club saw fit to take all the players to Northern Ireland for a friendly, and the windows in the team bus were smashed. During the match, one of the locals came at me with a boulder so big that he couldn't have thrown it more than two feet. The game was then stopped, and the players watched the supporters fighting each other while the police tried to intervene. To cap it all, someone threw a transistor radio onto the park, and Mark Reid thought that it was a bomb. I had never seen him run so fast as he bolted out of its way.

Thankfully, things seem to have changed for the better across the water. I go to Ireland about twice a year, and the tension has all but disappeared. That has had a knock-on effect for Scotland, in that we no longer import that tension via the fans who regularly come over to Glasgow to see both sides of the Old Firm.

No fixtures were cancelled after Doyley died. We played against Hibs at Easter Road the following week, but none of us were up for it, and it was no surprise when we lost 1–0. But that was our first domestic loss of the season. The four Old Firm games would be crucial as always, and we got off to a decent start on that front. We won the first meeting 2–0 on 19 August, then on 21 November we drew 3–3 at Celtic Park after Gordon Dalziel gave them an early lead with a peculiar diving header from about two inches off the ground. However, we lost the New Year Old Firm derby on 9 January, with Jim Bett scoring a penalty, although, in some ways, that match was just of local interest. Our main threat remained Aberdeen. Rangers had won the League Cup by beating Dundee United in the final, but they were still not good enough or consistent enough to challenge for the championship.

The draw for the 1982 World Cup in Spain was also made at the turn of the year, and Scotland were placed in the same group as Brazil, New Zealand and Russia, but I never gave it a second thought. I knew that there would have to be a plague before I was called up by Jock.

On 13 February, Aberdeen knocked us out of the fourth round of the Scottish Cup with a John Hewitt goal, which meant the pressure on us to retain our title increased. Our hopes took a knock when Charlie Nicholas sustained a leg break that would keep him out for the rest of the season. A few days later, I was playing around on his crutches in the dressing-room when someone said, 'You better not do that or you will end up with a broken leg, too.' I scoffed, 'Don't talk rubbish.' However, a couple of weeks later, I too was out for the rest of the campaign with a broken leg. Less than a fortnight after I celebrated my 26th birthday, Dundee United keeper Hamish McAlpine caught me as I was going through on goal at Tannadice. I thought that he could have pulled out after clearing the ball, but he followed through on me. I was determined not to let him know that I was hurt and tried to play on. I thought I just had a bruised muscle, but the ball came to me again, and I collapsed trying to chase it. Brian Scott, our physio, came on and told me I had broken my fibula. As I lay in hospital getting my leg put in plaster, I was unhappy with McAlpine, but there was a case for thanking him. It was during my break away from football that I decided to own up to my gambling problem and seek help.

Selling my new car to raise money for yet another big race meeting was the last straw. After the profits from the sale had been donated to the bookies, I realised that I still needed a car to get around. My Uncle Tommy, who stayed near Parkhead, had a car from the early 1960s, and he sold it to me for about £100. It was an utter embarrassment, and I hated driving it. People would stare at the car, but not in admiration. I spent all my time trying not to get caught driving it. I would park well away from Celtic Park and walk to the ground. At traffic lights, I would pretend that I was tying my laces in case I was noticed by the driver in the next lane. But people eventually got to know that it was mine. Having to drive around in that car was probably one of the biggest embarrassments of my life, but it symbolised the chaotic mess I was making of things.

We always paid the mortgage and bills, but I was constantly in debt. Pauline was aware of my gambling, but we didn't really argue a lot. She was more frustrated with me because she knew

I wanted to build up a property portfolio, something to keep us when we retired. Thankfully, the kids didn't miss out on anything. I was in the bookie's during the day when they were at school, and I didn't gamble at night, so I spent a lot of time with them. Pauline was good with money, and the kids always had birthday parties and good Christmases, so from that point of view they were unaffected. Nevertheless, I was frittering away money that could have been put to better use.

Thankfully, I didn't have a credit card, which I'm sure would have exacerbated my problem, but I was always looking for money. In a pub one night, I borrowed £20 off a guy whom I didn't really know but who turned out be a full-time hard man and a part-time money lender. I went back to give him the money the following week, and he said, 'You owe me £80. I give my money out at 200 per cent. If you don't give me it until next week, then you'll owe me £240.' I had no option but to give him £80. That frightened me enough to keep me away from his clutches in the future, but I was still always looking for quick money to gamble.

If people needed tickets for games, I would take money for them, which would fund an afternoon in the bookie's. I would ask Jim Kennedy in the Celtic ticket office to arrange to take the money for the tickets out of my wages. It was a helter-skelter way of managing your finances.

By this time, Pauline knew that my gambling was affecting me badly, and she was 100 per cent behind me as I sought to do something about it. I went to see my doctor, who advised me to contact Gamblers Anonymous. I stared at the telephone in my living room for ages before I eventually dialled the number. A friendly voice asked me to go along to a meeting that night in the council halls in Maryhill Road, close to Partick Thistle's ground. Pauline drove me over, she parked outside and we sat in the car. I was terrified and ashamed. How had it come to this? I had battled all my life to be a success as a footballer.

I was a winner, but the only way I could beat my gambling addiction was by admitting defeat.

Eventually, I plucked up the courage to go in, taking a deep breath as I gently knocked on the door and entered. Everyone was sitting at a big table, and I nervously sat down at an empty chair. They probably all knew who I was, but I looked around at a table full of strangers. They were mostly male but of all ages and all classes. I had to stand up and say, 'My name is Frank, and I'm a compulsive gambler.' I had never felt so vulnerable and alone.

There is no magic formula at GA. There are no potions or medicines. It is all about sharing your experiences with others. One guy spoke for a few minutes about his life, and I thought, 'My god, his life is identical to the one I'm living.' It was a horror story, but mentally and emotionally I identified with it. I was feeling everything he was feeling. From being alone minutes earlier, I now felt close to everyone in the room.

Everyone who uses the service has a different story to tell, but the same battle against addiction underpins them all. Fighting an addiction is a serious business, but there are the occasional humorous moments, too. When gamblers stop going to the bookie's, bingo or casinos, they find themselves with excess time on their hands, and GA advises taking up a hobby to fill the void. One man came to a meeting for the first time in weeks and was asked if he had found himself a hobby. He said, 'Yes, I bought a greyhound.' Everybody collapsed with laughter.

My initial involvement with GA was a success, and I stopped gambling for about six months and got my finances in order. I told Peter Benny, a London accountant and friend of my Uncle Frank who lived in Manchester, what was happening to me because of gambling. He couldn't believe it, which made two of us. I needed money. Badly. Peter had a meeting with Desmond White, who agreed to give me a £10,000 interest-free loan. Desmond was a complete gentleman. He never mentioned it to me, and the money I owed was simply deducted from my wages. I paid some debts and bought a new car, which I proudly drove into Celtic Park every day, hoping as many people as possible would notice it.

GA gave me simple hints to control my urges – apart from the obvious, such as not going to the bookie's. I was told not to buy a newspaper so I wouldn't know which horses were running. That was easy enough, but they also told me to stay away from people who liked a bet, which was a bit more difficult. Of course, there was no way I could tell the other players that I was at GA. I was too embarrassed to do that, and I prayed that they wouldn't find out from the press. I went from being at the hub of the card schools on the team bus to looking out of the window all the way up to places such as Aberdeen. If nothing else, my knowledge of the Scottish countryside increased.

We didn't lose a game after the day I broke my leg against Dundee United, and a 3–0 win over St Mirren at Parkhead on the last day of the season gave us our second championship in succession. Billy McNeill's management skills in overcoming the loss of his two top scorers was to be admired as he notched up his third title in four seasons against two of the all-time great managers in Scotland. My personal feud with Fergie had subsided, but I was still happy that Aberdeen had to make do with a Scottish Cup win over Rangers.

I wasn't bothered about missing out on the 1982 World Cup in Spain. My focus was off the park. For the first time in years, I felt in control of my life. I was attending a GA meeting most nights, and the remarkable people I was meeting were a great source of inspiration to me. Frank the non-gambler, the good guy, was back in town. Pauline and I were getting on fine. She was glad that I had been taking steps to cure my addiction. I was making plans for the future, and I dreamed again of getting my property business up and running. I looked forward to a life without gambling.

9

CHARLIE ISN'T MY DARLING

Normally, I enjoyed taking my family abroad for our summer holidays, but our trip to Portugal in 1982 proved to be a nightmare, especially for Pauline. The hotel next to us was still being built, and dust swirled across the boundary fence every day. At times, we had to leave the premises to find some fresh air. Pauline struggled with her breathing, which we put down to the circumstances, but when she returned she was diagnosed with asthma.

I was in better shape ahead of pre-season training. Charlie and I both made full recoveries from our broken legs, and we resumed our partnership at the start of the 1982–83 season. George McCluskey, one of the most skilful strikers ever to wear the hoops, was more often than not left on the sidelines. He admitted later in the campaign that it had been 'a bit of a wasted season' for him, which was a backhanded compliment to the form of me and Charlie. George still made a significant contribution, and between the three of us we scored over 100 goals that season.

Charlie had emerged as the golden boy at Parkhead, and, to be honest, I knew I couldn't reach his standards. He was an exceptionally gifted player, and in his two full seasons at Celtic he could have played for any team in Europe and not looked out of place.

Paul McStay broke through that season and became a great player, but Charlie was special, and I don't say that about many footballers. Paul quickly settled into the side, helped by the experienced players around him, but I didn't go overboard about him in the way that many fans and pundits did. He was intelligent, a good passer of the ball, and he could make and score goals, but he never had the pace to be special. I did feel sorry for him in the latter stages of his career when he was carrying a poor Celtic team, but he certainly enjoyed himself when he first came into the side.

Charlie had great technique, he could strike the ball with great power and direction, and he was an accomplished finisher. We complemented each other well. I was the one who went in behind defences, while he dropped deep to search for the ball. If one of the centre-halves went with Charlie, I would be left one on one with the other centre-back, and it just needed one good pass and I was through on goal. If Charlie's marker refused to be pulled out of position, he would have carte blanche to pick up the ball, turn and take on the defence, and there was nobody better in Scotland at that than him.

Although we got on well on the park, we weren't best buddies off it. He was a bit younger than me and would go out with guys like Danny Crainie, while our little social group of Roy Aitken, Davie Provan, Mick Conroy and me was well established. Danny McGrain would give Charlie a run to training, so they were very friendly, even though they were vastly different characters. It was said that when Kenny Dalglish was at Celtic, Danny would always look to pass to him, and that became apparent with Charlie as well. Danny would always try to give the ball to Charlie, even if I was in a better position. He didn't attempt to hide it, either. We played a friendly against Feyenoord in Holland, and Danny played a ball into the box from which I scored. As we made our way back for the restart, I said, 'Great pass, Danny,' and he growled, 'It wasn't for you. It was for Charlie.'

At least Danny would pass to someone. Charlie only passed in an emergency. You've got to have a big ego when you are a striker, but Charlie's was bigger than mine, and that's saying something. I wanted to score at least 20 goals a season, but if I thought a teammate was in a better position – and it was usually Charlie who was that teammate – I would not hesitate to set him up. But I thought Charlie was a more selfish player. In the two years or so that we played together, I can only remember him making one goal for me, and even then I'm sure he passed it because he thought that he would get the ball back again. It was against Hibs at Easter Road, and you can see it in the video of the match: he played me in at the edge of the box, and his arm was quickly out signalling for me to give him the ball back. He didn't seem too pleased when I buried it.

Charlie preferred to use me as a decoy. We played Motherwell at Fir Park early in the season, and he used me as a decoy three times, beat the same player three times and then hammered the ball into the roof of the net. What could I say? I'm sure our teammates, such as Murdo MacLeod, Roy Aitken, Paul McStay, George McCluskey and Davie Provan, would all agree that I was much more of a team player. Billy certainly recognised my worth to the team. He left me on the bench one day to play Charlie and George together, and it didn't work. He called me into his office on the Monday and said, 'Frank, I won't drop you again.' He could see that Charlie and George were too much alike – skilful players who liked to get the ball to feet – whereas I could stretch a defence and create space for my partner.

As the season went on, Charlie became increasingly interested in his social life and was perhaps out more than he should have been as a professional footballer. It was difficult for him. He was a young superstar who hadn't been taught how to handle fame, and I think it went to his head a bit. Socialising was becoming more important to him than football. You had to be a great trainer to socialise the way he did, but Charlie wasn't the most enthusiastic at Barrowfield.

We knew Celtic were going to cash in on him eventually, but, like most people, I was a bit surprised that he chose to go to Arsenal, especially when Liverpool were interested in signing him. Maybe he thought that he wouldn't get a game at Anfield, although I think that he just fancied being in London, and he certainly took to the social scene down there like a duck to water. He made his money by going to Highbury, but although his form was good at times he probably never reached the heights he had at Celtic, and I wasn't surprised that he didn't fit into George Graham's football philosophy.

I still occasionally hear fans arguing about the respective merits of Dalglish and Nicholas. Charlie was special for two seasons, Kenny was special for around twelve, and that is the big difference. But before Charlie departed for the bright lights of London, he contributed to some great Celtic performances and some memorable matches during the 1982–83 season.

We had a great start to the campaign with a 6–0 win over Dunfermline in the League Cup group stages, and we scored seven in the corresponding game at East End Park, nine in the two games against Alloa and seven in the two games against Arbroath. We really believed we could be on the brink of something special. Our first real test was against Ajax in the

European Cup, and, against the odds, we passed it with flying colours. The first leg at Celtic Park in September, which ended in a 2–2 draw, was one of the finest games I played in.

I almost had to pinch myself as I watched Johan Cruyff, by then thirty-five and back at the club he led to three European Cups, warming up before the game. The memories of the 1974 World Cup came flooding back, and I could not believe that the substitute for the Glasgow Amateurs Under-18 Select was sharing a pitch with the Dutch master. Not that he was a one-man team. Ajax were a magnificent side, with players such as Søren Lerby, Jesper Olsen and Jan Mølby in their ranks, and they had youngsters Marco Van Basten and Frank Rijkaard on the bench.

Billy had warned me that Lerby, who would be marking me, was quick, so when I got a chance at the start of the game I made my mind up to hit my shot immediately, but I snatched at the ball and missed. I looked round, and Lerby was six yards away. I just hoped that another opportunity would come my way before the end of the game.

I was mesmerised by the way Cruyff glided around the pitch, a pass here, a lay-off there, and all the time with space and time to call the shots. After only four minutes, Jesper Olsen flew past Danny McGrain and Davie Moyes before shooting beyond Packie in goal. I feared the worst, but the crowd got right behind us, we upped the tempo and there was bedlam ten minutes later when Charlie equalised from the spot after Cruyff had hauled down Tommy Burns to concede a penalty.

To their credit, Ajax showed no signs of wanting to settle for a draw, and in the 18th minute Cruyff took a pass from Olsen and played in Lerby, who chipped over Packie. Again, we refused to capitulate. It was unlike a typical European game, and the fans were loving it. I was dragging Lerby all over the pitch as the two teams went at it hammer and tongs, and I had a feeling that another chance would come my way. Three minutes before half-time, it did, and I slotted the ball into the net from close range. The crowd gave both teams a standing ovation as they left the pitch at half-time.

The second half was goalless, and the scoreline made Ajax favourites to progress. By the way they bounced off the pitch, their players clearly thought that the second leg was a formality. We still harboured hopes of going through, but we couldn't have envisaged what was to happen when we travelled to Amsterdam. Although Ajax had two away goals, I'm not sure that they quite knew how to approach the game: whether to go for the win or hold onto the draw that would see them go through on the away-goals rule. We certainly knew we had to score at least one, and the breakthrough came in the 34th minute when I played a one-two with Charlie and he knocked it past Dutch international goalkeeper Piet Schrijvers, who had been replaced by Hans Galjé for the first leg after injuring himself in the warm-up.

That sparked Ajax into life, and when they equalised through Gerald Vanenburg it looked like they had done enough. They took Cruyff off, although not before he had broken the nose of Graeme Sinclair, who had been assigned to man-mark him. We took chances as we went for the winner, but it was clear that the Dutch side were toiling, and we finished the game stronger. Late in the second half, Sinky moved up the right-hand side and crossed a brilliant ball into the box, but although my header beat the goalkeeper it hit the underside of the bar, bounced on the line and spun back into his arms. I thought that was our chance gone, but we kept going and got our just rewards with only a couple of minutes remaining.

There were shades of the 1980 Scottish Cup final when Danny McGrain took possession of the ball outside the Ajax box and tried to shoot, only to see the ball spin to George McCluskey. George was the calmest man on the pitch as he placed the ball into the far corner of the net. The Ajax players could not believe that we had snatched a late winner, and we celebrated wildly with the fans who had travelled over to support us. Neil Mochan pulled a muscle as he leaped from the dugout to acclaim the goal. It was the first time in a decade that we had beaten a major European side, and we had achieved victory the Celtic way: by attacking our opponents. It was also the first time in a decade that all four Scottish teams had survived the first round in European competition. One reporter said it had been 'the best performance by a Scottish side on foreign soil apart from 1967 and 1972', referring to Celtic's European Cup win and Rangers European Cup-Winners' Cup victory.

After disposing of one of the European heavyweights, Real Sociedad, our opponents in the next round, held no fears for us. We were more defensively minded in the first leg in Spain, and for about an hour they weren't a threat, but Jesús Satrústegui and Pedro Uralde scored to give us a mountain to climb in the second leg. I had played well, and we had been applauded by the Real fans after the game, but it was no consolation.

We knew it was going to take a big European night at Parkhead to turn the tie around, but after Pedro Uralde scored for them in the 26th minute, it was all but over. We had about nine players back for a corner, but their lone attacker somehow managed to find space. It was poor defending again, and it pissed me off. We had to score four goals to go through, and that was too much. Murdo MacLeod equalised soon after and scored again in the 89th minute, but the tie was well over by then.

The win over Ajax had not propelled us on in the way we had hoped. Before the second leg against Sociedad, we drew with Dundee United and lost to Aberdeen, although on 30 October, four days before our European exit, we beat Rangers 3–2 at Parkhead in the first Old Firm game of the season. On 13 November, Charlie scored a hat-trick in a 5–0 win over St Mirren that put us six points ahead of Rangers. Our old rivals were almost out of the title race, and it wasn't yet December.

Meanwhile, I had returned to gambling with a vengeance. GA had been good for me in the first few months, but I didn't have a strong enough desire to quit for good. And when someone tells you they have started gambling again, they mean they have started losing money again.

Pauline was very supportive. She joined GamAnon, a group for partners of people struggling with a gambling addiction. She made friends with other people who knew what she was going through. I could tell when Pauline was attending GamAnon meetings and when she wasn't. I think she coped better with me – and life in general – when she attended meetings on a regular basis.

I was one of several Celtic players who went for a pint in Glasgow's Chevalier Casino after a Wednesday night game, and, as usual, I quickly lost what money I had on me. At about 11.30 p.m., I went out to the hole in the wall to withdraw £50 – the maximum at the time. I was back in the casino within minutes throwing it all away. My teammates had disappeared home, so I could not borrow any money to chase my losses. I realised that it was past midnight and nipped back out for another £50. It wasn't long before I had lost that as well. I had enough for a fish supper, but as I came out of the chippy, I thought, 'Sod it. I'll go back and chance my arm at the bank again.' I put my card into the machine, and, as on the previous two occasions, the hatch opened up. But this time I had an unopened fish supper in my hand, and with nowhere to put it I sat it inside the hatch. I tried for another £50. On the third unsuccessful try, the screen informed me that there were no more funds available, and the machine confiscated my card. Before I realised what was happening, the hatch closed over, trapping my fish supper inside. I half-expected a little rain cloud to follow me back to my car. I had to drive home skint and starving.

CHARLIE ISN'T MY DARLING

Normally, I enjoyed taking my family abroad for our summer holidays, but our trip to Portugal in 1982 proved to be a nightmare, especially for Pauline. The hotel next to us was still being built, and dust swirled across the boundary fence every day. At times, we had to leave the premises to find some fresh air. Pauline struggled with her breathing, which we put down to the circumstances, but when she returned she was diagnosed with asthma.

I was in better shape ahead of pre-season training. Charlie and I both made full recoveries from our broken legs, and we resumed our partnership at the start of the 1982–83 season. George McCluskey, one of the most skilful strikers ever to wear the hoops, was more often than not left on the sidelines. He admitted later in the campaign that it had been 'a bit of a wasted season' for him, which was a backhanded compliment to the form of me and Charlie. George still made a significant contribution, and between the three of us we scored over 100 goals that season.

Charlie had emerged as the golden boy at Parkhead, and, to be honest, I knew I couldn't reach his standards. He was an exceptionally gifted player, and in his two full seasons at Celtic he could have played for any team in Europe and not looked out of place.

Paul McStay broke through that season and became a great player, but Charlie was special, and I don't say that about many footballers. Paul quickly settled into the side, helped by the experienced players around him, but I didn't go overboard about him in the way that many fans and pundits did. He was intelligent, a good passer of the ball, and he could make and score goals, but he never had the pace to be special. I did feel sorry for him in the latter stages of his career when he was carrying a poor Celtic team, but he certainly enjoyed himself when he first came into the side.

Charlie had great technique, he could strike the ball with great power and direction, and he was an accomplished finisher. We complemented each other well. I was the one who went in behind defences, while he dropped deep to search for the ball. If one of the centre-halves went with Charlie, I would be left one on one with the other centre-back, and it just needed one good pass and I was through on goal. If Charlie's marker refused to be pulled out of position, he would have carte blanche to pick up the ball, turn and take on the defence, and there was nobody better in Scotland at that than him.

Although we got on well on the park, we weren't best buddies off it. He was a bit younger than me and would go out with guys like Danny Crainie, while our little social group of Roy Aitken, Davie Provan, Mick Conroy and me was well established. Danny McGrain would give Charlie a run to training, so they were very friendly, even though they

We beat Dundee United over two legs in the League Cup semi-finals to set up an Old Firm final at Hampden, where we gathered the first piece of silverware of the season. In driving rain, Charlie scored a fantastic opener at the Celtic end, his low drive from the edge of the box taking Rangers keeper Jim Stewart by surprise as it sped past him. Then Murdo cracked one into the roof of the net, and at half-time we were cruising. Jim Bett scored for Rangers after the interval, but we ended up deserved winners.

On 8 January, when Murdo scored in a 1–0 win at St Mirren, it was our 100th goal of the season. We already had nine Scotland internationals in the squad, Murdo was just about to start his Scotland career and Packie was a Republic of Ireland player. We had every right to be confident. However, the occasional blip was costing us. A week later, Brian McClair scored twice for Motherwell to beat us 2–1, and in doing so probably won himself a move to Parkhead the following season.

But we bounced back. I scored a double in a 4–1 win over Hibs, and in a 3–0 Scottish Cup win at Clydebank we had a four-man strike force of Nicholas, McGarvey, Provan and McCluskey. We still thought that we were on course for the Treble, but the Premier League had twists and turns galore before the end of the season.

We drew again with Dundee United at Tannadice in February, this time 1–1. The following week, we lost 3–1 at home to Aberdeen, which knocked us off the top of the table for the first time in 25 months. Eric Black scored a hat-trick for the Dons, while Charlie got our goal. Aberdeen were now one point ahead of us, although we still had a game in hand. Most people believed it was another race between Aberdeen and Celtic for the title. Few thought that Dundee United, four points behind Aberdeen and three behind us, had a chance of actually winning their first league crown. The three teams were neck and neck, and Rangers, although out of the title race, were capable of taking points from anyone on a one-off basis.

When you are a striker and scoring goals, you enjoy your football, and I was certainly having fun that season. I scored two against Dunfermline in a 3–0 Scottish Cup win at Parkhead and two against my lucky side Kilmarnock at Rugby Park. I then notched again as we hammered Hearts 4–1 in the Scottish Cup. With Aberdeen still going strong in the European Cup-Winners' Cup, it was all heating up nicely for a dramatic climax to the season.

The second half of March was disastrous for us. We lost 2–1 against Dundee United at Tannadice then drew 0–0 with Rangers. A 1–1 draw against St Mirren at Celtic Park on 27 March saw us drop back behind Aberdeen by a point after they had beaten Morton. There were just two points between Aberdeen, Celtic and Dundee United, and it was anybody's guess who was going to win the title.

I scored in a 3–0 home win against Motherwell, and with seven games remaining we were back on top by one point. A 2–0 win over Dundee United at Parkhead the following Wednesday was followed by a 3–0 win at Easter Road. We were handed an unexpected favour by Rangers when they beat Aberdeen 2–1 at Ibrox on the same day, but Dundee United's 2–1 win away from home to St Mirren kept the pressure on.

However, as quickly as we had found our best form, we lost it. The Scottish Cup escaped into the distance when Aberdeen knocked us out of the semi-finals, and four days later we slipped up against Dundee United at home, a turning point in the campaign.

It was an epic game against the masters of the counter-attack, although strangely witnessed by only 23,965 fans. Paul Hegarty gave United the lead after 14 minutes before Charlie Nicholas scored from the spot. Eamonn Bannon put United ahead again with a penalty seven minutes after the interval, and we were struggling until Richard Gough was sent off. When Tommy Burns scored to make it 2–2, that should have been enough for us. We just needed to see the game out, but we went for the winner. Even with ten men, United cut through us, and Ralph Milne scored to give them a crucial win.

Billy got it wrong that night. We should have been content with the point, but, to be fair to him, it's difficult to stop a team's momentum in those circumstances. The fans at Parkhead want you to push forward all the time, and that's why Celtic get lots of late goals; however, that mentality can occasionally cost you dearly, and that's what happened against United.

A 1–0 defeat at Pittodrie in the league the following Saturday thanks to a Mark McGhee goal was our third blow in a row. Dundee United leapfrogged us by a point with a 4–0 win against Kilmarnock. It was the first time United had topped the table, and with four games to go, although it was still neck and neck, the pendulum had swung their way. United matched our 5–0 win at Kilmarnock with a 4–0 win at Morton. We had two games remaining, one of them an Old Firm encounter at Ibrox.

On 7 May, we beat Morton 2–0 at Parkhead, but United hammered Motherwell 4–0 at Tannadice. With one game to go, three teams were in with a chance of winning the league, and there was a possibility that the title could go to a play-off for the first time in the history of Scottish football. If Dundee United drew 2–2 and Celtic won 4–2, it would be a dead heat. If Celtic drew and United lost, Aberdeen would win the title if they beat Hibs. It was that close.

We were playing at Ibrox, and Dundee United were playing at Dundee, while Aberdeen, who had won the Cup-Winners' Cup against Real Madrid in midweek, were playing at Easter Road. It could hardly have been more tense.

I was confident of going to Ibrox on the last day of the season. We had the measure of Rangers at that time, and they were frightened of us. I was more worried that the title wasn't in our hands, as I thought it likely that Dundee United would beat their neighbours. The afternoon started badly, as we found ourselves two goals down after 23 minutes. On top of that, we could tell by the reaction of the Rangers fans that United were ahead. We didn't know that they had scored two goals in eleven minutes, Ralph Milne and Eamonn Bannon having both netted.

At half-time, despite Aberdeen being on their way to a 5–0 win over Hibs, United were effectively the champions. But there was a memorable moment when we came out for the start of the second half. Far from being despondent, the Celtic fans were singing at the top of their voices, while the Rangers supporters were silent. You would have thought that we were winning. That gave us such a lift. Charlie Nicholas scored a penalty four minutes into the second half, and we were back in the game. Tam McAdam equalised just after the hour mark, and I then out-jumped Peter McCloy to head us into the lead. The Rangers fans just sat there in silence. Another Nicholas penalty four minutes from the end of the game – that's right, two penalties for Celtic at Ibrox in an Old Firm game – gave us the victory we deserved. But when the final whistle went, we discovered that it wasn't enough. United, on fifty-six points, were champions by two points over Aberdeen, who had beaten us on goal difference.

Aberdeen then beat Rangers 1–0 in the Scottish Cup final, which meant that the three domestic trophies had gone to three different teams, none of them from Govan. Scottish football had never been so competitive, and it hasn't been since. Not everyone was happy with the way the season had ended. Despite having his first European trophy under his belt and a Scottish Cup to boot, Fergie slaughtered his players live on television just after the final whistle at Hampden. He always has been a hard man to please.

Jim McLean had proved himself to be a magnificent manager, and he thoroughly deserved to win the title, his achievement all the more remarkable given that he used a squad of about 14 players. Winning the championship with so few players will probably never be replicated. McLean ran Tannadice with a rod of iron, and anyone with any interest in Scottish football has heard the stories of how and why he would discipline his players. However, when you consider the number of players who have gone into coaching after leaving Dundee United, it shows that they must have learned something from their manager.

In the close-season of 1983, we learned that Charlie had been sold to Arsenal behind Billy's back. But was Charlie leaving Parkhead the making of me in the way that the newspapers made out? No. I played exactly the same way regardless of who was my strike partner. It was just that I was noticed more. I wasn't resentful, but there had been too much attention on Charlie, to the detriment of the other players.

There was no surprise when Billy followed Charlie out of the door, although his destination of Maine Road in Manchester raised a few eyebrows. It was a poor decision by the board to allow him to go, and it was all the more distasteful that the spat was carried out in the press. It wasn't the first time, and it wouldn't be the last time, that the Celtic directors had failed to treat their manager with the proper respect. Jock Stein rejuvenated the club, won nine titles in a row and the European Cup, and made the club a fortune, yet he was not invited onto the board after he left Celtic Park.

If the Celtic board had given Billy more money to strengthen the defence – and the contract he was looking for – we could have pushed on the following season. In the five years between 1978 and 1983, he had won three Premier League titles, a Scottish Cup and a League Cup. With a better defence, it could have been more. Billy was always battling for more money, but the club were reluctant to fork out, especially on defenders.

I still maintain that if we had strengthened our defence, we would have definitely won a European trophy again. You defend as a team and attack as a team, so we all have to take the blame for losing goals, but the defence could have done better in important games.

I don't think Celtic got the best out of Roy Aitken by playing him in defence. He was very strong in midfield, where he should have been used, but because we didn't have enough good centre-backs he had to be deployed at the back. Roy was played as a sweeper behind Tom McAdam, who was essentially a striker. Danny McGrain was coming to the end of his career, and Mark Reid at left-back was average. By contrast, Aberdeen had Jim Leighton, Stuart Kennedy, Alex McLeish, Willie Miller and Doug Rougvie, and Dundee United had Hamish McAlpine, Richard Gough, Dave Narey, Paul Hegarty and Maurice Malpas, two sets of defenders that would underpin not only domestic success but success on the European front. Why wouldn't the Celtic board go that extra mile?

Fergie leaving St Mirren was devastating, but I coped better with the departure of Billy. I had become more experienced about the peculiar ways of football, which didn't always make sense to the players or fans. I was also confident that I would be able to impress whoever came in to take Billy's place.

10

MAKE HAY ANNOYED WHILE THE SUN SHINES

Like most of the Celtic players, the first I knew that Davie Hay was to be our new boss, and only the club's sixth manager in its history, was when I read about it in the morning papers. Davie was only 35 at the time and had been out of football for a year after leading Motherwell to the First Division title in 1981–82. He was working in the pub that he owned when the Celtic board made their approach.

I knew all about Davie Hay as the highly respected former Celtic, Chelsea and Scotland player. He had been one of the 'Quality Street' gang that Jock Stein had brought through the reserves, and, like his teammates Kenny Dalglish and Lou Macari, Davie had left the club to move to pastures new in England. He could play in defence or midfield, and I could still picture his long-distance drive that almost brought a goal against Brazil in the 1974 World Cup. He might not have been the most experienced candidate available, but his playing pedigree was sound, he had links with the club and he had the more experienced Frank Connor as his assistant.

However, I didn't know Davie as a person. Our paths hadn't crossed, and we hadn't met socially. But I think he took an instant dislike to me, which, as the old joke goes, might have just been him saving time. Nevertheless, it resulted in our relationship not being as good as it should have been, and I certainly did not enjoy as close a bond with him as I had with Billy.

When we flew out on a pre-season tour to Switzerland and Germany, I was nursing a stomach injury that couldn't be diagnosed properly by Brian Scott. I could run and do most other things in training, but I couldn't lift my right leg to shoot. It was frustrating, and we couldn't get to the bottom of it. Although I couldn't train properly or play in the games, to all intents and purposes I was fine, and, like all the players, I would sunbathe during our free time. However, Roy Aitken, Davie Provan and a few of the other players wound our new boss up by suggesting that I was swinging the lead. 'Frank is just over for the holiday, Davie. He'll let you know when he's ready to play,' was an example of one of the comments that was made. This went on for days, and eventually I had to say, 'Guys, you need to stop. This is getting up Davie's nose. I'm struggling with this injury.'

But Davie took the bait, and I was ordered to train by myself one morning at 9.30 a.m., which wasn't great, given that the card schools were going on through the night. I played my last hand at 8.45 a.m. and then went to my room to get changed. Davie trained me for an hour at the side of the hotel until I dropped, and while I suffered the other players were hiding in the bushes having a laugh at my efforts. A few days later, the injury disappeared as quickly as it had surfaced. But I don't think Davie trusted me after that. I wasn't worried about my place in the team, but it wasn't the start I wanted with a new manager.

While the Celtic players adapted to the new methods of Davie Hay, the fans were adjusting to the loss of Charlie, although Rangers supporters were certainly glad to see the back of him. We lost the Old Firm Glasgow Cup final at Hampden to a Sandy Clark goal, and throughout the game the Rangers fans sang 'Where's your Charlie gone, where's your Charlie gone?' to the tune of the old pop song 'Chirpy Chirpy, Cheep Cheep'.

Charlie's replacement was Jim Melrose, the former Partick Thistle striker, who was bought from Coventry for £100,000. Later in the campaign, Brian McClair arrived from Motherwell, costing £75,000, and before their arrival most Celtic fans and players could not have separated the two in terms of ability. However, the differing fortunes of both men exemplified how difficult the step-up to the Old Firm could be for players.

Some people find playing for Celtic too much to cope with, and Jim was one of them. The fans didn't really take to him, and they gave him a lot of stick at times. You could sense his frustration, and it all came out when he scored a goal against Dundee United and gave a 'get it up ye' sign to the fans. That wasn't a good idea. Once you have gestured provocatively to the fans, you're finished. You can't do that to the people who pay your wages, and Jim lasted only a year before he moved on.

There have been a lot of players like Jim who couldn't quite do it at the top level. John Halpin, one of the boys who came through the youth system during my time at Parkhead, was a good player on his day, but he wasn't consistent. He had a good game then a bad game, and in the end he wasn't up to it and had to move on. John Colquhoun arrived from Stirling Albion later in the season for about £60,000 to put pressure on Davie

Provan, but Davie was miles better. John couldn't cross a ball, whereas Davie would put it right on your head. John was a decent player, as he showed when he moved to Hearts, but he was not Celtic class.

McClair, however, was the club's top scorer for the next four seasons before leaving for Manchester United. He was a quiet, studious sort of guy who kept himself to himself, but he turned out to be a great buy. He had a great engine and could play in attack or midfield. Wherever he played, he was great at getting himself into the box at just the right time.

However, Brian would be the first to admit that he was nowhere near as good as Jimmy Johnstone, who returned to the backroom staff at the beginning of the season. That was a bit of an eye-opener for us all and a great thrill for guys like me who had worshipped him when we were growing up. He played in five-a-side games with us, and even though he was about 40 years old at the time we couldn't get the ball off him. He must have been magic to play alongside in his prime.

We got our revenge over Rangers at Parkhead in the first Premier League Old Firm meeting of the season on 3 September, and once again I helped myself to a late winner against our big rivals. It was the one and only time that my grandmother Hannah, a wonderful woman, came to see me play. I had said to her before the game, 'Granny, if I score today, it's for you.' We got off to the worst possible start when a young stripling called Ally McCoist scored after about thirty-three seconds, but Roy Aitken got the equaliser about seven minutes later, and I scored with approximately four minutes to go. Davie Provan nearly kicked Peter McCloy's face off going for a loose ball, and it broke to me about seven yards out. I just struck it as hard as I could, and it just missed John McClelland's leg before hitting the net, allowing Granny Hannah and more than 40,000 Celtic fans to go home happy.

A week later, I scored in a 5–2 win over St Johnstone at home and went off before the end to a standing ovation. A newspaper article the next day claimed that I was 'no longer playing in the shadow of Nicholas', which annoyed me somewhat. As far as I was concerned, I had never played in the shadow of anyone.

Jock Stein, however, might well have read that match report before he brought me back from the international wilderness for a friendly game against Uruguay at Hampden on 21 September – or it might have been several call-offs from a game that hardly fired the imagination that lay behind his decision. Jock, a former Celtic centre-half, said to the press, 'I wouldn't like to have played against Frank,' which was a compliment to my form at the time, but, if anything, I had played better in previous seasons. Nevertheless, after four years out of the international scene, I was back in the squad.

I started up front with Kenny Dalglish, who was earning his 91st cap, while Paul McStay made his debut. But it again ended in frustration for me. After only 17 minutes, I sustained an injury in the nether regions that required six stitches after a challenge by goalkeeper Rodolfo Rodríguez. There were just over 20,000 there to see Scotland win 2–0 thanks to a first-half penalty by John Robertson and a goal from my replacement Davie Dodds ten minutes after the break. It was so demoralising. While my Celtic career was almost at its peak, my Scotland career refused to take off.

I kept my place in the squad for the European Championship qualifying game against Belgium at Hampden on 12 October but had to be content with a place on the bench, coming on for Charlie Nicholas with 16 minutes to go when it was 1–1, Charlie having scored our goal. I was on the bench again for the trip to East Germany for the next qualifier on 16 November, coming on for Paul McStay after an hour in a 2–1 defeat. All that way for half an hour's game time. Where was the glamour of international football? East Germany was such a drab place, and I remember the SFA officials on the bus to the airport after the game gathering all the local money, which couldn't be exchanged outside the country, and giving it to the bus driver, who thought he had won the lottery.

A Home International against Northern Ireland in Belfast on 13 December was my next port of call, and this time I started before being replaced by Mark McGhee after an hour. Dalglish, Nicholas and Archibald, all playing in England, had – surprisingly – withdrawn. Norman Whiteside and Sammy McIlroy scored in a 2–0 defeat that was termed an 'embarrassment' by the Scottish press.

The following February saw Wales travel up to Hampden for our Home International meeting, and again I was hooked just after the interval, this time for Watford striker Maurice Johnston, who would soon be my teammate. In front of just over 21,000 fans, we beat Wales 2–1, Maurice scoring the winner after Leighton James had equalised Davie Cooper's first-half penalty, and although I didn't know it at the time my international career had come to an ignominious end.

European football for Celtic that season was to be in the shape of the UEFA Cup, and we were handed a relatively easy tie against Danish side Aarhus. We struggled a bit in the first leg at home, relying on a Roy Aitken goal to give us a narrow win, but in the return leg a fortnight later we cruised to a 4–1 win, with me, MacLeod, Aitken and Provan on the scoresheet.

It looked like our European adventure was going to be short and sweet when we lost 2–0 to Sporting Lisbon in Portugal, their star man Jordão scoring a double. It was the worst European performance by Celtic in my time at the club. Sporting should have won 6–0 in Lisbon, and they must have flown to Glasgow thinking, 'This mob are hopeless.' Consequently, they went into the game too relaxed. Before the match, our dressing-room was quiet with everybody concentrating on what we had to do. There was a full house that night, and as soon as they took the centre we went after them. They didn't know what had hit them. We set up attack after attack, and we were soon 3–0 up through goals by Tommy Burns, Tom McAdam and Brian McClair. Murdo MacLeod scored just after the break, and I grabbed the fifth. Sporting were punch-drunk and could have lost by more. It was one of the club's greatest ever European victories and also one of my best games for Celtic.

When I rejoined St Mirren, manager Alex Miller said to me, 'I was at that game against Sporting Lisbon. Were you all on something that night?' It was simply determination that drove us on. A packed Celtic Park can give you an extra yard of pace, and when you have nothing to lose and everything to gain you just go for it. Sporting, on the other hand, went into the match with the wrong attitude and paid a heavy price.

We were paired with Brian Clough's Nottingham Forest in the next round, a 'Battle of Britain' draw that whet the appetite of the media and supporters. Although past their European Cup-winning best, Forest were still a more than decent side. Thousands of Celtic fans packed into the City Ground on a freezing cold night to see us hold out for a deserved goalless draw. It wasn't a game with many chances, but we more than held our own and looked forward to the second leg in Glasgow. Many observers thought that the hard work was done, but the Celtic players didn't think that the tie was over. Forest were comfortable defending and adept at hitting on the counter-attack. They had been all over Europe in previous seasons picking up results against some of the best clubs on the Continent, and, of course, they had a football genius for a manager.

Clough was unorthodox in many ways, but when he spoke you listened. He never missed a trick and would do anything to get an edge, however inconsequential it might seem. Davie Hay still had his pub in Paisley, and Clough directed the Forest team bus there on arriving in Scotland. He ordered drinks for all his players and told the bar staff that Davie would pay for them. It was Clough showing that he was the one calling the shots, and if that confidence transmitted itself to his players even a little, then it was worth it.

The onus was on us to take the game to Forest, but it became clear early on that they were composed, patient and made of sterner stuff than Sporting Lisbon. Steve Hodge and Colin Walsh scored for them, and although Murdo pulled a goal back we were well beaten in the end.

While Celtic, Aberdeen and Dundee United fought for the title again that season, Rangers continued to struggle, and we watched with interest from the other side of the city. As early as 17 September, after Rangers lost to Aberdeen at Ibrox to leave them in eighth position in the league with one point from their opening eight games, the press claimed that the 'Greig Must Go' chants had begun. The natives were not happy. McCoist and Cooper, according to reports, were made to run a 'gauntlet of hate' after they lost 2–1 to Motherwell at home on 22 October, even though McCoist scored a penalty. Inevitably, Greig was sacked. He had found it problematic making the transition from player to boss, but he was also unlucky that his first step into management had coincided with Alex Ferguson, Jim McLean and Billy McNeill all coming to the fore at the same time.

Ferguson and McLean both had the chance to take over at Ibrox, but both declined. That was a huge blow to Rangers, who had historically been able to attract the very best talent to the club, apart from, of course, those who were Catholic. Although not the only reason for knocking back a move to Ibrox, it has subsequently emerged that neither man was comfortable with what Rangers represented at that time. The club's anti-Catholic practices had come back to haunt them. They could have signed me for about £100, and I would have scored a lot of goals, but it seemed that I was rejected because of the school I attended. What was all that nonsense about?

Jock Wallace returned in November, and in his first game back in charge Rangers lost 3–0 at Aberdeen. Nobody was surprised. The malaise was deep. Unlike most Celtic fans, I wasn't glad to see them struggling. I couldn't have cared less. I was only concerned about Aberdeen and United. Although Rangers had good players, including Davie Cooper and Bobby Russell, they weren't up to the mark, and we had the measure of them.

We usually beat them with some ease at Parkhead – a once-in-a-lifetime Alex Miller drive notwithstanding – and playing at Ibrox wasn't a problem for us. We were not intimidated. We had a team packed with experienced players who were mentally strong. I liked to walk out with Roy beside me, because, like me, he wasn't scared of anything, and when you looked down the line in the tunnel and saw players such as Danny McGrain, Tommy Burns, Murdo MacLeod and Davie Provan you knew it was going to take a good team to beat you. On top of that, Ibrox did not create an intimidating atmosphere while it was being rebuilt.

On the other hand, I always felt that more than a few Rangers players were intimidated at Celtic Park. Great player though he was, Davie Cooper didn't like playing in front of the Jungle, just yards in front of Celtic's most fervent fans. I use a boxing analogy when describing the balance of power between the Old Firm. When two boxers go into the ring, one knows deep down that he is superior, while the other is less confident. When I played for Celtic, we felt superior to Rangers.

On the Saturday after we had thrashed Sporting, and with Rangers coach Tommy McLean temporarily holding the fort at Ibrox, we travelled across the city and showed our superiority with a 2–1 win, Tommy Burns and me getting the goals in what was one of four Premier League wins in November. December saw us drop a point against Aberdeen and Dundee United, games either side of a victory over Hearts at Tynecastle, which saw the locals venting their spleen at me. John Colquhoun made his debut for us in a 3–1 win, and the Hearts fans were so incensed by the prospect of defeat that I had to run from a shower of coins as I made to take a corner. The police moved in to restore order, but it was the Hearts supporters who took a note of my name for future reference.

Unfortunately, the championship began to slip away from us. When Aberdeen beat us 1–0 at Pittodrie at the beginning of February, they went six points clear at the top of the table. However, we got revenge of sorts in the semi-final of the League Cup when we knocked them out over two legs to set up a meeting with Rangers at Hampden.

An incident during the build-up provided me with a little bit more evidence that Davie Hay was perhaps not my number one supporter. We stayed in Seamill before the final, as was tradition, and the day before the game a few of the Catholics in the team went to Mass. At the team talk later in the day, Davie went round the players, praising them and trying to build their confidence. He said, 'You always battle your corner, Murdo. Let's have the same again, and we will have no problem.' Then to Roy he said, 'They don't like playing against you, Roy. Don't you forget that.' When he came to me, he said, 'I noticed that you went to Mass, Frank. I hope you said, "Forgive me father, for I have sinned. I had a nightmare last week."' A few of the players giggled, and it could have easily been construed as a throwaway line or Davie attempting to inject some humour into the meeting, but it was no laughing matter to me. I thought that he spoiled the moment by having an unnecessary dig at me. Players need to be built up before big games not brought down, and it made me think that my days at Celtic might be numbered.

There was to be no divine intervention in the final at

Hampden when we were beaten 3–2 after extra time. That was the day that Ally McCoist should have been accepted by the Rangers fans, who had given him a lot of stick since his arrival from Sunderland. My hat-trick against St Mirren was my defining moment in terms of being recognised as a Celtic player, and Ally could do little more in the League Cup final to show Rangers fans that he was up to the standards required at Ibrox. He had a penalty saved by Packie Bonner but followed it up to score the winner, so it looked like his luck had changed as well. But even when he was getting stick from Rangers fans thereafter, I knew he would come good. He was a good player with a great personality.

Another comfortable 3–0 home win over Rangers at the beginning of April at Celtic Park kept us in the title chase, and we didn't lose another league game that month, except for a 1–0 defeat at Ibrox, our first loss to Rangers in four league games that season. That same weekend, a 2–0 win for Aberdeen at St Johnstone kept them four points ahead of the chasing pack and needing only five points to win the title. They were not to be denied. The championship was sewn up against Hearts with four fixtures in hand. The Dons finished the season seven points ahead of us and ten ahead of Dundee United, who were a further five ahead of Rangers. It was an impressive and emphatic achievement, and you couldn't deny that Fergie had taken another step to greatness.

The Scottish Cup final offered us a chance to finish the season on a high as we faced up to our new foes Aberdeen, playing their third final in a row, having won the previous two against Rangers. It had been another painless route to the final for us. We had beaten Berwick Rangers 4–0 away in the third round, before hammering East Fife 6–0 at Bayview. Another 6–0 win, this time over Motherwell at Fir Park, sent us into a semi-final against my old side St Mirren, which we won 2–1.

We knew that if nothing else the game against Aberdeen

would be a physical test. Some of the players Fergie had brought into the Aberdeen first team were hard pros who pushed referees to the limit. They kicked lumps out of you, and Willie Miller was a prime example. He was Player of the Year and Players' Player of the Year that season, and his ability was not in doubt, but he got away with a lot, and I think he should have been sent off more often. In one game, I skinned Alex McLeish and was right through on goal before Miller pulled me back. He didn't even get booked. I was going off my head, but the referee was more inclined to send me off for complaining than he was to deal with Miller.

Aberdeen had perfected the art of putting referees under pressure, and it paid dividends. Fergie's players would surround the referee when they felt aggrieved, and once a referee is surrounded he can be intimidated. I know it may sound ironic coming from an Old Firm player, but I always felt that Aberdeen would get the benefit of the doubt. They certainly had no fears about coming to Ibrox, Parkhead or Hampden and fighting their corner, and the final on 19 May was another ill-tempered affair.

There was little to choose between the sides in the first half, but Eric Black gave Aberdeen the lead after 23 minutes from what seemed to be an offside position, and things looked bleak for us when Roy Aitken was sent off after he clattered into Mark McGhee. It wasn't a great tackle, but it should only have been a yellow card. However, the Aberdeen players were on the case of referee Bob Valentine from the first whistle, and Roy consequently became the first player to be sent off in a Scottish Cup final since Rangers' Jock Buchanan in 1929. We kept going, pushed on by the fans, and with four minutes to go Paul McStay equalised. For a few minutes, we thought that we would have the momentum to get the winner, but Aberdeen made the extra player count. After eight minutes of extra time, substitute Dougie Bell drove a shot that struck the junction of post and bar, Gordon Strachan crossed to the back post, Packie came out flapping and Mark McGhee drove home from a tight angle. We were shattered, but more importantly we were trophyless. Davie Hay's first season in charge at Parkhead had seen Celtic finish runners-up in the league, League Cup and Scottish Cup. It was good – but not good enough.

11

· ·

THE GOAL

If I had a penny for every time someone stopped me to talk about my winning goal against Dundee United in the 1985 Scottish Cup final at Hampden, I would be a millionaire. Or at least have a good few bob. There were about 50,000 Celtic fans in the ground that day, with millions more watching on television, and I seem to have bumped into them all, at least once, over the years. Like me, they have great memories of that day: how we fought back from a goal down to equalise from a Davie Provan free-kick; my late winner; and how, in their own ways, they celebrated later that night. The fact that it was the 100th Scottish Cup final made it even more special.

When punters ask me to recall the goal, I usually reply, 'I tripped over my laces, and the ball hit my head and went into the net,' and it gets a little laugh. I don't say it was all about experience, concentration, timing and getting a great connection on Roy Aitken's cross, even though that is closer to the truth. When Roy charged down the right-hand side, I knew that he would put the ball in early, and I had only one thought: to get in the box. The United defenders held a decent line, but I was quick and got in between them. As soon as I headed the ball, I knew it had a chance, but I didn't see it hit the net, as I fell awkwardly. I was disorientated for a split second, but the thunderous roar told me all I needed to know. I looked up and saw the Celtic fans going mental, and I ran towards the main stand and dropped to my knees. It was the most wonderful feeling: an eruption of joy, happiness and, to be honest, relief.

On my living-room wall, I have an iconic picture of me wheeling away a second after scoring, and when I look at it I am transported back to that day. The standing ovation I received from the Celtic fans after scoring the second goal of my hat-trick against St Mirren was my best moment in football, but my cup final goal comes a close second. I should have retired from football after that game. In fact, come to think of it, I did – as a Celtic player, at least.

We had a fantastic party at the Grosvenor Hotel in Glasgow afterwards, and I basked in the glory of being a cup-final hero. The champagne was flowing, the players were congratulating me on winning them the big bonus that guaranteed a good summer holiday and there was a good old-fashioned sing-song. Davie Hay and I were cuddling each other. I knew and he knew that I had saved him from the sack. Defeat against United would have meant two seasons without a trophy, and that is not acceptable for a Celtic manager. But the pressure was off him, and I thought that there would have been enough gratitude on his behalf for him to give me the new deal I wanted. As the night continued on in fine style, I thought, 'Davie owes me big time. I will speak to him on Monday morning while he is still on a high.'

160

I was certainly still buzzing when I drove into Parkhead on the Monday morning. I knocked on Davie's door, entered and told him that I wanted to see him about a new contract. Right away, I felt uneasy. Davie's beaming smile from Saturday night had gone, replaced by an anxious look. He stopped me in my tracks by saying, 'Next season I am looking to play Brian McClair and Mo Johnston up front and to bring Alan McInally through.' I was taken by surprise. I hadn't seen that coming, and it took me a few seconds to gather my thoughts. 'McClair, Johnston and McInally?' I thought. I could have accepted McClair and Johnston, but not McInally. That was an insult. Alan was a decent player, but I could guarantee Celtic at least 20 goals a season – McInally couldn't.

Almost as an afterthought, Davie offered me the same wages with a £1,000 signing-on fee. I said to him, 'It's obvious that you don't want me to stay,' and he replied, 'That's right.'

My head was spinning. How could he do this to me? I had won the Scottish Cup for Celtic two days previously and had almost certainly kept him in a job. I was just 29 and had again scored more than my fair share of goals that season. Surely I should have been shown more respect after what I had done for the club since signing five seasons previously? At that moment in time, I was a Celtic hero. But heroes are not always afforded the respect due to them at Parkhead. I had witnessed that ten months earlier as we prepared to win back our title from Aberdeen.

On 4 August 1984, we played Arsenal at Parkhead with Charlie Nicholas appearing for the Gunners. We beat them 3–2, but the real story was the treatment of Nicholas, who was booed throughout the game by Celtic fans unhappy that he had left the club. He endured the same treatment as Kenny Dalglish when he had returned after signing for Liverpool. I think Celtic supporters are great, but they were a bit over the top giving Charlie stick. All I can say to them is that if they were on £300 a week, would they have stayed at Parkhead instead of going to London for six or seven times that amount? In my opinion, Charlie had no option but to go, and Celtic made a lot of money from a player they had brought through the ranks. Everyone was a winner, except, of course, the supporters who take it as an insult if any player leaves their favourite club. Charlie gave Celtic fans a lot of memorable moments, and he was a great player in his two seasons in the first team. It wouldn't have been a hardship to give him a round of applause. He said in the press that he'd expected the reception he had received, but he would not be human if it had not hurt him a bit.

In typical selfish striker's mode, I quickly forgot about the treatment of Charlie. I was more worried about my early form, failing as I did to find the net in the first five games of the 1984–85 season. Draws against Hibs, Dundee United and Rangers at the start of the campaign put me and the team under pressure. Thankfully, I got off the mark in the league when I scored twice in a 5–0 win over Morton, but a 2–1 defeat against Dundee United at Tannadice set us back, and a 1–1 draw with Dumbarton at Boghead had Davie Hay describing us as a 'disgrace', although I had scored our goal, so I exempted myself from the criticism, as all good strikers do. I notched again in a 1–0 home win over Hearts, and we moved into third place in the table behind Aberdeen and Rangers with wins over St Mirren and Dundee.

Our next task was to recover from a 1–0 first-leg defeat by Ghent in the first round of the European Cup-Winners' Cup. We took care of business on a typically rainy night in Glasgow. Right from the first whistle, we laid siege to their goal, but we had to wait until just before the interval until I broke the deadlock. Just after the break, I grabbed another to put us ahead in the tie, but with the visitors needing just one goal to take them through on the away-goals rule there were plenty of nerves around until Paul McStay added a third.

We didn't lose a game in October. I scored against Aberdeen in a 2–1 home win, and before the 3–0 home win over Hibs Maurice Johnston joined us from Watford for £400,000. I was happy to see him come, because I knew he would strengthen the side, but for the first time in my Celtic career my place was really threatened. It was clear that Maurice was a diehard Celtic fan. He was the player featured in the club programme later in the season when we played Dundee in a Scottish Cup quarter-final replay at Celtic Park. According to Mo, the high point of his career was signing for Celtic, the low point was Celtic not signing him from Partick Thistle, his best goal was his first against Rangers, his favourite player was Kenny Dalglish, his favourite stadium was Celtic Park and his favourite other team was Celtic Reserves. I always wondered if he had a twin brother who later played for Rangers. However, I was one of the few people who was not surprised when he was paraded as a Rangers player a couple of weeks after it looked like he was returning to Parkhead in the summer of 1989.

A former teammate told me in the February that David Murray had met with Mo in a Paris restaurant, where it was agreed that he would sign for Rangers in July. I told a few friends who then told a few of their friends, but, of course, most people didn't believe the rumour. I wasn't surprised. After all, it was potentially the biggest story in Scottish football, but I was confident that it would happen. I believe the whole thing was set up by Rangers to get one over on Celtic, and it certainly worked. If Mo did know that he was signing for Rangers, I have to wonder why he allowed himself to be paraded at Celtic Park for the second time holding the Celtic jersey.

I got on great with Mo when we were together at Parkhead, and he liked playing up front with me. He was very good in the air, a great finisher, very hard-working and unselfish – unlike Charlie. Indeed, when Mo was at Partick Thistle, Davie Provan and I told John Kelman, the chief scout at Celtic, that the club should look at him, but they waited until he had moved to Watford and then had to pay big money to bring him back to Scotland.

We beat Dundee United at the end of month to pull within one point of our new adversaries Aberdeen, with Mo scoring his first goal for the Hoops to set us up for the first leg of our European Cup-Winners' Cup second-round tie against Rapid Vienna in Austria. The game was a tougher than normal European tie but gave no indications of what was to follow in the return game at Parkhead. Alan McInally was sent off in Vienna, and I nearly picked up the second broken leg of my career in a ridiculous tackle by a nutter called Reinhard Kienast, but, to a certain extent, we had coped comfortably enough with what they had to offer. Although we had lost 3–1, Brian McClair's goal meant we were confident that, with the crowd behind us at home, we could get through to the next round.

Not one of the 48,000-plus crowd who filed into Celtic Park for the return leg will ever forget what they witnessed. Rapid didn't fancy it at all. We could see that in the early stages of the match. We stormed into a 3–0 lead thanks to goals by Brian McClair, Murdo MacLeod and Tommy Burns before the game descended into farce – a farce that ultimately saw us knocked out of the competition following one of the biggest miscarriages of football justice.

The Rapid players had not been slow to put the boot in, but it all kicked off after Tommy went in hard on their keeper Kjell Johansson. Retribution took place and Kienast, the nutter who had tried to maim me in the first game, was sent off for punching Tommy.

When we were then awarded a penalty after their keeper had fouled Tommy, all hell broke loose. The referee went to consult with his linesman, and missiles began to be thrown from the Jungle. One of their players, Rudi Weinhofer, fell to the ground clutching his head, although the nearest bottle had landed yards away from him. I would have laughed if I had not realised how serious the situation was. I was first over to Weinhofer, and there was no damage to him at all. Of course, Vienna tried to milk the situation for all it was worth, and Weinhofer ended up so heavily bandaged that it looked as though he was wearing a turban.

I hadn't been involved in a game that had such an air of lawlessness about it. Their skipper, the famous Austrian international striker Hans Krankl, wanted to take the Vienna players off the pitch, but, after minutes of confusion, they eventually agreed to play on. Amid all the petulance and bad feeling, and with the crowd baying for blood, Peter Grant missed the penalty, although I don't know why, with all the noted goal scorers on the pitch, he was allowed to take it. It was a strange feeling when the final whistle ended the game. We knew we would be in trouble but had no idea that UEFA would make such a mess of their investigation.

At first, UEFA found Weinhofer's claim to be unfounded. Celtic were fined £4,000 for the behaviour of the supporters in the Jungle, and Vienna were fined £5,000, but the result was to stand, and we were thus through to the next round. We thought that was the end of the matter, but how wrong we were. Rapid appealed, claiming that Weinhofer had actually been struck by a coin, and another UEFA committee doubled Vienna's fine but declared the second game void. It would have to be replayed. The players were shocked. We had no idea how they could arrive at such a decision. Not only had we to play the second game again, but we had to play it at least 100 kilometres away from Glasgow.

Desmond White should have withdrawn the club from the tournament on receipt of UEFA's decision. I liked Desmond – he had always looked after the best interests of the club and he had been good to me – but the one mistake he did make was to validate UEFA's mess by agreeing to play again. In my opinion, withdrawing and accepting the consequences would have been a more dignified response to what was a clear injustice.

But, as always with Celtic, the loss of revenue from failing to go through to the next round was their biggest concern. Also, most people at Celtic thought that we would beat Rapid Vienna again, regardless of where we played them. They hadn't looked great under pressure at Parkhead, and it was thought that overturning a 3–1 deficit for a second time would be easy enough. Celtic accepted Manchester United's offer to play the game at Old Trafford, knowing that the supporters would travel down in their thousands and that there would be enough local interest to guarantee an almost full house.

I felt uncomfortable about it all. If I had been a stronger character at the time, I would have told the Celtic board that I didn't want to play at Old Trafford. But you did what you were told as a player. If they had ordered us to play in Australia, the players would have complied.

There was a poisonous atmosphere around Manchester on the day of the game, even though it was played around five weeks after the match at Parkhead. The city had been invaded by around 40,000 Celtic fans, and I could sense the hatred emanating from the ones we passed as the bus made its way to the stadium. To be honest, I was consumed by the same hatred. We all knew we had been cheated.

Old Trafford was meant to be a neutral venue, but it was a sea of green and white, with almost no Austrians present. The Celtic fans were psyched up and aggressive, and for the first time in my life I had butterflies in my stomach before the match. It had turned into more than a game of football. But it all fell flat. Instead of the huge Celtic travelling support spurring us on, we seemed drained. It was too much to ask for another 3–0 scoreline, and by beating them at Celtic Park we had lost the element of surprise. Rapid had been bitten once, and they were better organised and obviously intent on simply defending their two-goal lead. Driven on by the crowd, we became anxious, yet, ironically, it was seconds after coming close to getting the breakthrough that we lost the only goal of the game.

After Roy Aitken had hit the post with a shot, Rapid picked up the rebound, and in a swift counter-attack the ball was shuffled to Peter Pacult, who skipped past Danny McGrain to go clean through on goal and score. To add to the sense of deflation, some needless violence further marred the night. Their goalkeeper was attacked by a fan inside the goal, and at the end of the game, as the players were coming off, one of their players was kicked by a Celtic fan who was being led away by police after being arrested. We were left thinking of what might have been. I am not the only Celtic player to still believe that if the result from the game at Parkhead had been allowed to stand, we would have gone on to win the competition.

It grated with everyone concerned with Celtic when Rapid made it all the way to the final, where they met Everton. I was never so happy to see a team beaten as I was to see Rapid lose that night. I loved it. Rapid Vienna cheated us at Celtic Park, and it still eats away at me. Even now, I find it hard to talk about it. I know that it may sound like an overreaction, but I don't like Austrians because of that game. I haven't met any since, and I don't want to meet any in the future. I still love to see Rapid Vienna lose. I'm always happy to see them knocked out of Europe, and I wish the club nothing but bad luck.

It took us a while to get over the Rapid debacle, but in the five weeks between the second-leg at Parkhead and the replayed game at Old Trafford we won four of our five league games, the 4–2 defeat by Aberdeen just before the trip to Manchester spoiling a good run that included 5–1 victories over Hearts and Dundee and a 7–1 win over St Mirren. The next game after Old Trafford was a 1–0 win at Hibs, but a 1–1 home draw with Rangers and a 2–1 defeat by Dundee United at Celtic Park made December a miserable month.

The New Year began with an Old Firm win over Rangers at Ibrox, but inclement weather meant that we didn't have another outing until the Scottish Cup third-round win at Hamilton Accies. Our league form was up and down, beating St Mirren 2–0 then losing by the same margin to Dundee. A 4–0 trouncing of Morton was followed by an even more encouraging 2–0 home win over Aberdeen.

But one step forward was followed by a step back, March beginning with a goalless draw at Dundee United, and a 1–0 loss at Hibs saw us fall eight points behind Aberdeen. It was too big a gap to make up, and we had to accept the fact that we were out of the title race for the second season in succession. Aberdeen effectively wrapped up the championship with a 1–1 draw with us at Pittodrie, although technically they still had to win another point. Fergie's intrusion into the Old Firm duopoly was proving to be much more than a flash in the pan. Aberdeen finished a healthy seven points ahead of us, with fifty-nine points, and twenty-one points ahead of Rangers, who had tied with St Mirren in fourth place. Rehiring Jock Wallace in the hope of returning the glory days to Ibrox had backfired. Rangers, despite winning the League Cup earlier in the season by beating Dundee United, had hit rock bottom.

The Scottish Cup was our last hope of a trophy, and, in all modesty, it was me who did more than most to get Celtic to the final. I was angry at being made substitute when we played at Hamilton in the third round. I was always angry when I was left out, but as far as I was concerned I was playing better than Brian McClair and Maurice Johnston at that time. Davie told me on the Tuesday that I wasn't playing, but he couldn't give me an explanation as to why, because there wasn't one. It was simply the manager's prerogative, and, like all players, I had to accept his decision.

I sat on the bench and fumed as we struggled in the first half, going in one goal down at the break. Davie then asked me to go on and do him a turn, and I duly scored both goals that took us into the next round. Those occasions are very satisfying for a substitute. By scoring goals, you are saying, 'I told you so,' without actually having to say the words.

I was also on the scoresheet in the next round when we hammered Highland League side Inverness Thistle 6–0 at Parkhead. It was the same weekend that a goal by Dundee midfielder and red-hot Rangers fan John Brown knocked our Ibrox rivals out of the cup, the fans turning on Ally McCoist with the infamous chant 'Ally, Ally, get tae fuck'.

There was no surprise when Brown ended up at Ibrox, but he could have worn the hoops. Davie Hay asked a few of us what we thought about him, and the consensus was that he was a good player and we should sign him. He was strong, determined, good in the air, versatile and was a goal threat, and he would have really helped our defence. It didn't matter what his background was; he would have signed for Celtic. Nobody from the smaller teams in Scotland knocks back a chance to play for one of the Old Firm clubs. I think even Ally would have gladly signed for Celtic that day the Rangers fans gave him stick.

In the quarter-finals, we had two chances to see Brown at close quarters, the 1–1 draw at Dens Park resulting in a replay at Celtic Park. Mo Johnston and I scored in a 2–1 win, which set up a semi-final meeting with Motherwell at Hampden. I was more than a little annoyed when I was again left out of the first game, which ended in a 1–1 draw, especially when I sat on the bench for the whole match. Even my teammates expressed surprise that I hadn't been thrown on near the end to try and grab the winner.

I was even more pissed off when Davie stuck to the same side for the replay. It was still goalless with 65 minutes gone when he once again asked me to go on and pull him out of a hole. I was more determined than I could remember, and I unsettled their defence, to the extent that Roy Aitken's goal and a Mo Johnston double eased us into the final. I met fans later who said that they knew we were going to win when I came on, which is the highest praise you can get from your supporters. I certainly needed a boost, because I wasn't getting it from the manager at that point in the season.

Dundee United, who had beaten Aberdeen in the other semi-final, were to be our final opponents, but in the run-up to the game I didn't think I would start in that match either. Indeed, I worried that I wouldn't even make the two-man bench.

Before a big game like a cup final you are always looking for signs or hints that you are in the manager's plans. When Davie sent a Celtic side to Manchester United the week before the final to play a friendly and I wasn't even in the squad, my mind went into overdrive. As normal, we set up camp at Seamill during the week, and I was included in the preparations, which was heartening, but some of my teammates were winding me up. Davie Provan kept saying, 'You'll be lucky to be in the squad for Saturday, Frank.'

I tried not to let it get me down, but the possibility of being left on the bench was running through my mind. It would have been a disaster for me, but I would have had to have put a brave face on it. As a professional, you can't go in a huff when you are left out. You have to think of the team, but it's not always easy. Everyone remembers Jim Leighton walking round the Wembley trackside after being dropped for the 1990 FA Cup final replay against Crystal Palace. He cut a forlorn figure, but he had to sit on the bench and be supportive of his club. Fergie was vindicated when United won the cup, but that would have meant nothing to Leighton.

Thankfully, I was spared a similar torture. The day before the game, Davie followed me into the toilet at the hotel and said, 'Just to let you know that you will be playing on Saturday.' He was fair to me in that respect. I think he knew that without my help Celtic would not have made it to Hampden. I often wonder, though, if he picked me knowing that I would probably not be at Parkhead the following season.

I had just turned 29 a couple of months earlier, and I wanted to finish my career at Celtic. As we warmed up, I was thinking, 'If I get a goal today and we win, I might get a new two-year contract.' I was confident of at least getting a year's deal. Celtic could depend on me scoring over 20 goals a season. Surely that counted for something?

I didn't do my chances of a new deal much good during a relatively uneventful first half. We couldn't get going as a team, and nothing was falling for me. The half-time whistle gave us a chance to regroup, but just ten minutes into the second half United midfielder Stuart Beedie caught us sleeping and fired them ahead.

We couldn't find a way back until Beedie was replaced by John Holt, a more defensive-minded player. Jim McLean wanted to hold onto the one-goal lead, but you couldn't do that to the Celtic team I played in. United needed a second goal. I mentioned in an article years later that McLean's substitution had given us a boost. He hit back, explaining why he had made the decision and saying that I was wrong. He was a brilliant manager, but I will say it again: it was the wrong decision.

To be fair, it didn't look that way as the minutes ticked away. However, our chance came in the 77th minute when we won a free-kick 25 yards from goal. I saw Murdo shaping to take it, but I thought that it was better positioned for Davie Provan. Murdo had a great shot, but Davie could put bend on the ball. Davie ended up taking it, and I was glad to see his magnificent free-kick flash past McAlpine. After that, there was only going to be one winner. The Celtic fans got right behind us and carried us on. We gained a yard, we were sharper and faster, and the belief drained out of the United players. All I needed was a half-chance, but it wasn't coming my way. I was beginning to think about the prospect of extra time when Roy drove forward and set me up to be the Hampden hero.

On the Sunday and Monday, the newspapers were all about me winning the Scottish Cup for Celtic, but in the following few days they confirmed the shock news that I had rejected Davie's offer and was to leave the club.

I have heard people say that he didn't want me to stay because of my gambling, but that wasn't the case. I was no better or worse than a few of the other players at that time, and it had no effect on my form. Davie's decision was made purely for football reasons, and he was being honest with me, something I respected, even though I disagreed with him. We have spoken about it since, and he has told me that, in hindsight, he should have kept me on for another year at least. I don't hold grudges – Rapid Vienna aside – and if Davie phoned and asked me to go for a pint with him, I would happily go.

In many ways, it was a great way to end my Celtic career. I can go to my grave saying that my last touch of the ball for my boyhood heroes was scoring the winner in a Scottish Cup final at Hampden. I'm happy with that.

12

···

A LOVE STREET REPRISE
AND THOSE JAMBO JIBES

Stunned as I was to be heading out of the door at Celtic, I knew I would have no problem getting fixed up with another club. Without meaning to sound big-headed, I was more than aware of what I could offer. I was a good goal scorer, but I also made goals for other players, and there weren't many of those types of players around. My forte was my work rate and my ability to get behind defences. If you ask any of the players who played for Celtic at that time, they would confirm that I got behind opposition defences more than any of the other forwards in the team. It was a hard, hard job, and it has become harder, because defences are better drilled these days. Consequently, most modern-day centre-forwards don't get behind the opposition back four, although for a lot of them this has nothing to do with coming up against better-organised defenders – it's just laziness. That's why I like Scott McDonald. He works hard to stretch defences and still scores goals, and Craig Bellamy did that as well in his short spell at Celtic Park.

I've heard all the jibes about my style of play, and I feel insulted by them. After the 1985 Cup final, Dave Narey trotted out the old cliché: 'Frank doesn't know what he is going to do, so what chance do we have?' Well, Dave, I knew what I was doing when I headed the winner past Hamish McAlpine at Hampden. Narey's remark was typical of those players who tried to get a cheap laugh because they couldn't cope with me, and over the years I've also heard various pundits trot out the same sort of stuff.

I don't know if I was unorthodox or not, but when I was in possession I wanted to keep the ball until I could get a shot in or set up a teammate. I detested giving the ball away, and I would do what I could to keep it. A lot of players take the easy option and cross the ball when they know they will hit the defender. Why do that? I would twist and turn to try and make a bit of room for myself. I would go to my left. If I was covered, I would go to my right, then my left again, and if there was still no way through, I would try something else. If that made me slippery, then so be it, but it didn't appear to bother my teammates – apart from one. In my first spell at St Mirren, Jimmy Bone complained to Ricky Macfarlane that he wasn't scoring goals because I was taking too long to get a cross in. All of the other strike partners Jimmy played alongside must have been the same as me, because he was never a great goal scorer.

I would find being a striker easier these days due to the changes to the pass-back rule. Willie Miller could knock the ball back to the goalkeeper, who could pick it up, and he would get a big round of applause from the fans. Nowadays, goalkeepers are not allowed to pick up the ball from pass-backs unless it is from a header or chest, and that has hampered defenders. They now have to concede a shy or a corner, and that puts defences under more pressure. I would have thrived on that uncertainty. In fact, I would love to see a new rule introduced where pass-backs are totally banned. That would make the game more exciting. I would also like to see the offside rule changed back so that offside is offside. There are too many grey areas concerning the 'second phase', which confuse referees and the punters.

Within days of being told that I was no longer wanted at Celtic, I was asked by journalist Ken Gallacher if I would be interested in going to Dundee United. (That was the way that a lot of transfers were conducted at the time. Journalists were used to sniff out initial interest before an official approach was made.) Jim McLean had obviously forgiven me for costing his side a Scottish Cup. However, great manager that McLean was, I quickly said no. United were a very good side, who at their best played wonderful, free-flowing football, but I didn't want to move to Tayside, which was a prerequisite for United playing staff at that time. More importantly, his reputation for dealing with players was controversial. The successful United players earned good bonuses, but they got a hard time from their manger for all manner of reasons. On one famous occasion, he docked his players money for not being entertaining enough after they had won a cup-tie 6–1. I was an experienced player who would have had difficulty adapting to the McLean style of management. I would undoubtedly have crossed swords with him at some stage, and that would have been sore on the pocket. I wasn't prepared to risk that. I have never actually spoken to Jim McLean, which is a shame, and if he had phoned me up himself, I would have given it more serious thought. The personal touch might have made a difference – but we'll never know.

Alex Miller, by then St Mirren boss, called to ask if I wanted

175

to return to Love Street. Our first meeting didn't go well. He offered me £100 per week less than I was on at Celtic and a £1,000 signing-on fee. I walked out. It was a classic case of a club trying to get a player on the cheap, even though Celtic were only asking £70,000 for me.

St Mirren eventually offered me a £23,000 signing-on fee and £275 a week, £90 less than what I was on at Celtic, and I accepted. It was a significant increase from their original offer, which I might well have grabbed had I been a younger player. My signing-on fee for St Mirren was more than both signing-on fees for Liverpool and Celtic combined. I have the feeling that would not be the case these days.

I bought a flat for £8,000 as an investment, but my future was being determined by my fondness for a bet. When I was gambling, I was gambling with the sort of enthusiasm that I displayed on the pitch. I took out a couple of loans on the strength of the property, and when I sold the flat a couple of years later, unsurprisingly, I made no profit.

Alex Miller told me that I would be playing in attack with Frank McAvennie, who had begun to make a name for himself at St Mirren. I thought that it would be a good partnership. Frank was hard-working and lively, and he could score goals. I didn't get long to speculate as to how our partnership would work in practice, as Frank signed for West Ham almost the day after I rejoined St Mirren. I still believe that Alex knew McAvennie was going to West Ham and that St Mirren had to secure me before he could let him go. The club had signed a player for £70,000 and sold one for £300,000, so, in that respect, it was a good bit of business but not a great start to my relationship with my new boss. However, Alex was, and still is, a good honest professional whom I respect, regardless.

He put a lot of emphasis on hard work and trained us more than Fergie did, but, like Jim Clunie, he was very defensively minded, and he wanted me to close down full-backs, which wasn't to my liking. I was getting older, and I wanted to use all my energy to create and score goals, so there was friction at times when Alex implored me to chase defenders down the flanks.

Alex could also get hung up on the opposition rather than letting them worry about what his side could do. He started a team talk before one game against Rangers at Love Street at 11.30 a.m. I had to meet somebody outside the main door at 1 p.m., so I thought that I had plenty of time. At 12.50 p.m., he was still talking about Rangers. Most of the players had switched off after about 20 minutes. There is only so much information you can take in. He noticed I was getting fidgety and said, 'What's up, Frank?' I replied, 'You've been talking about Rangers for over an hour.' He said, 'Yes, you're right, Frank. It's not about them. It's all about what we do. Right, lads, off you go.'

There had been lots of changes at Love Street in the six years I had been away. Tony Fitzpatrick, Campbell Money, Billy Abercromby and Mark Fulton were the only players left from my first spell there. The new crop of players included guys such as Stevie Clark, Tommy Wilson, Peter Godfrey, Neil Cooper, Brian Gallagher, Gardner Speirs, Jim Rooney and Dave Winnie. Paul Lambert would not break through until the following season, and Ian Ferguson had yet to arrive from Clyde. Kenny McDowall was my strike partner on and off, as was Paul Chalmers, son of Lisbon Lion Stevie Chalmers.

Several players, such as Stevie Clark, Tommy Wilson and Kenny McDowall, are still involved in the game in a coaching capacity. Kenny was a good professional but a very quiet guy, not one for shouting and bawling on or off the pitch. On the other hand, Billy Davies, who signed for St Mirren after we won the cup, was a moaner who hated me moaning at him. Billy was a good player but would just hold onto the ball a

177

wee bit too long at times. He also went into coaching and management, so it shows that it takes all different types.

Although we won the Scottish Cup in my second season back at Love Street, the first St Mirren team I played in were far superior in my opinion. Fergie's side was packed with good players, most of whom moved on to bigger clubs. Iain Munro was one of the fittest players in football. I found it hard to keep up with him at training but that kept me pushing to improve. In my honest opinion, and in the opinion of many who knew him, Bobby Reid was the best centre-half in Scotland, but an injury that he picked up in a Scotland Under-21 match put him out of the game, which was a crying shame. He would have been a Liverpool player along with me if he had not been so unlucky. I'm sure of that, and I'm certain a long career with the full Scotland team awaited him.

As a striker, I was fortunate to have Tony Fitzpatrick, Billy Stark and Lex Richardson behind me in midfield. I was assured of a good supply of the ball. Tony was wise beyond his years, and although he didn't score a lot of goals he did a fantastic holding job. He was captain by the time he was about 20, which I thought was incredible, given that at that age I was a skinny wee guy from junior football looking to establish myself in the team. When I left for Liverpool, Tony moved to Bristol City, but it was only lack of pace that prevented him becoming a great player and finding a top club.

Big Starky arrived at St Mirren at the same time as me after being released by Rangers, and he was a really nice guy. He was tall, skinny, and a great passer and striker of the ball who got his fair share of goals. He had an unusual way of running that made some St Mirren fans think he was lazy, but he could get up and down the right-hand side, and he made me a lot of goals. He followed Fergie from St Mirren to Aberdeen, which is an indication of his quality. Billy McNeill signed him for Celtic, and Starky ended up as coach there working under Tommy

Burns. He deserves everything he gets from football, and it's great to see him working with the Scotland youth set-up. Lex was an underrated player but not among his teammates. He could get about the pitch, and he set me up with more than a few goals. Above all, it was such a joy to play football under Fergie, and that was important to me.

After leaving Celtic, I knew my career was on the wane. There was no doubt about it. Nevertheless, I believed I could add to my medal collection at Love Street. Maybe some of the magic of Fergie had rubbed off on his brother Martin Ferguson, Alex Miller's assistant. The club had reached five semi-finals in the previous five seasons, so a cup win was a real possibility, although we had not won the Scottish Cup since 1959 and hadn't won the League Cup at all.

The Premier League title was way out of our reach, but, as it transpired, we did have a significant part to play in deciding its destination during the 1985–86 season. Our opening-day 2–1 defeat at Dundee wasn't the best start, but in front of the St Mirren fans at Love Street the following week I marked my return with a goal in a 6–2 hammering of Hearts. I was given a great reception and named Man of the Match. It could hardly have gone better, and the next day one newspaper said, 'When even the opposing fans get excited when a player touches the ball, he has to be special, and that was Frank McGarvey.' The reporter was confusing the Hearts fans' excitement with vein-bursting vitriol, which had become a feature of what was a special relationship between them and me – and worse was to come. Alex Miller called me a 'magic pro', which was a boost as I set about adapting to life away from Celtic.

My private life remained unsettled. I was drifting in and out of gambling. My home life was happy when I abstained and not so happy when I was in the bookie's. I knew that I should have been doing something more positive with my money – my family's money. But at times I was helpless to stop.

One of the uplifting moments was the birth of our third son, Scott. I received a call at 3.40 a.m. informing me that the birth was imminent, but although I drove as fast as I could to Rottenrow Hospital, where I had been born, I was too late. I was disappointed, because I was keen to be with Pauline at the birth, but the important thing was that my wife and child were both healthy, and I had been lucky again.

St Mirren's involvement in the UEFA Cup was a bonus, and there was less expectation at Love Street than at Celtic Park, which, in its own way, made the games more enjoyable. The first round against Slavia Prague was relatively straightforward. The approach to European football at that time, if you were drawn away in the first leg, was to 'keep the score down' to give you a chance in the return match in front of your own fans. That was our attitude on our trip to Czechoslovakia, and we were relatively successful, losing by just one goal. We didn't bank on the return game at Love Street going to extra time after we could only get past their defence on one occasion through Brian Gallagher, but it allowed me to become the hero of the night when I scored twice. I was especially pleased with my second goal: a little back-heel flick from a Kenny McDowall cross. However, I wish I hadn't said to the press, 'It is the sort of thing every school kid tries, and being ahead there was no pressure on me. A lot of people think it was brilliant – and I think they are right.' The dangers of speaking while drunk on adulation have never been more evident.

Ironically, St Mirren had lasted longer than Celtic in Europe, my old club going out to Atlético Madrid after failing to overcome a 2–0 first-leg deficit in the return game at Parkhead – in a match played behind closed doors as further punishment following the Rapid Vienna debacle. I told the press that I didn't take any satisfaction from the result, and I meant it. I bore no grudges against Celtic. I was quoted as saying, 'Certainly, I don't like to think that I've taken some kind of revenge because Celtic wanted rid of me. The people who will suffer most because of that defeat by Atlético are the people I like most: the players and the supporters. I feel very sorry for them.'

I didn't actually realise how strong my feelings were for Celtic until we played them the following Saturday. If our next fixture hadn't been at Parkhead, I would have missed out, because I had taken some rough treatment against Slavia Prague, and I was far from 100 per cent fit. But I was desperate to go back and score to show the fans what they were missing and to show Davie Hay that he had made a mistake in letting me go. Instead, I left Celtic Park embarrassed and ashamed after failing to give my all for a club for the first and only time in my career.

It was an emotional return to Celtic Park, and as we lined up just before kick-off the whole Jungle started singing 'There's only one Frank McGarvey'. I gave the fans a wave, and they let out a huge roar. I had never heard that before – they had booed Dalglish and Nicholas when they had returned, albeit under different circumstances. After that, I lost my concentration and found it difficult to give my all. I was thinking about my son, who was in among the Celtic fans, the cup-final goal at Hampden against Dundee United and the letters I had received from Celtic supporters when I had left the club, and it was all too much for me. I was playing for St Mirren, but I could hardly face the prospect of scoring against Celtic. How could I do that to the supporters who were singing my name? I could have gone off, but that would have made things worse.

In the end, we lost 2–0, and I received good marks in the newspapers the next day, which eased my guilt a little. However, deep down, I knew that I hadn't given 100 per cent, and I am still embarrassed about it. Maybe it's a tactic that Celtic supporters should use in the future when one of their former players returns to Parkhead? All I know is that I was glad when the game was over, and recalling it still makes me feel uncomfortable.

St Mirren could have drawn Real Madrid, Inter Milan or AC Milan in the second round of the UEFA Cup, but instead we found ourselves facing Swedish side Hammarby. The first leg in Sweden ended in a 3–3 draw, Brian Gallagher scoring a hat-trick for us, and with three away goals the tie had swung in our favour. I opened the scoring at Love Street, which meant, of course, that they had to score twice to win. Alex Miller took me off near the end, and the fans gave me a great ovation. Alex was delighted, as were the rest of guys in the dugout, and he was shaking my hand, slapping my back and saying, 'Well done, Franky boy. That was a great game you played. In you go for a bath.' I trotted up the tunnel, glad to get use of the hot water before everyone else. I was just putting my shirt on, thinking about who we would get in the next round when the dressing-room door opened and Alex came in. He looked like he had just seen a ghost. I didn't actually ask him the score or anything like that. I just said, 'Are you all right?'

He replied, 'We got fucking beat.'

'What do you mean we got beat?' was the best response I could muster while my brain tried to make sense of his statement.

'They scored two late goals.'

I couldn't believe it. We had been cruising when I had come off, but we had managed to lose two goals in the last two minutes. Some fans had left the ground early thinking that St Mirren had won the tie. There were only a few Hammarby supporters at the match, so I hadn't heard any cheering in the dressing-room. It wasn't until later that I heard that they had actually scored another goal that had been disallowed. It was one of the most astonishing European defeats suffered by any Scottish club. I don't think Alex ever recovered from that game. I don't think the players or fans did either.

Our season dwindled away after that, and our performances away from Love Street were especially poor. From being a club high on confidence, we went into free fall. Having been dumped out of the League Cup by Dundee United in September, Hearts then put us out of the Scottish Cup in March.

One irate fan complained in the programme for the match against Hibs on 29 March that he had only seen St Mirren win five points away from home all season. Another supporter urged the club to open a gate at Love Street for unemployed fans to boost the crowds that had dropped to only 3,000 at times. It was all very depressing, and the players just wanted the last game of the season – against Celtic at Love Street on 3 May – out of the way. Like the majority of clubs in the Premier League, we had nothing to play for on the last day of the season except a win bonus. We would finish seventh in the table, but there was no relegation that year anyway, as the league was being extended to 12 clubs the following season.

Unfortunately for us, our opponents were still in the hunt for the title, although it looked an unlikely prospect as they travelled along the M8 to Paisley. The championship was out of Celtic's hands. Hearts had only to win at Dens Park that day and they were champions. Even if they lost, Celtic had to beat us by at least four goals.

We should have known that it was going to be a difficult day when we lost our keeper to illness just before kick-off. At two o'clock, Campbell Money reported ill, and Jim Stewart was told that he would have to play. Half an hour later, someone was being violently sick in the dressing-room toilets. We looked in to see who it was and discovered that it was Jim. It wasn't the best preparation, but all the while we still presumed that ultimately the game would be meaningless.

We started well enough and missed a couple of decent chances that might have floored Celtic, but they basically ran riot after Brian McClair scored in the sixth minute, and there was nothing we could do about it. Maurice Johnston scored two in a minute around the half-hour mark, and Paul McStay got another before the break. We sat helpless in the dressing-room, knowing that the momentum was with Celtic. McClair scored another ten minutes or so into the second half, and the attention turned to the match at Dens Park, which was still goalless. Seven minutes from time, there was a big roar from the Celtic fans after news came through that Albert Kidd had put Dundee ahead. Four minutes later, they were going mental when Kidd scored again. The final few minutes were unbelievable, Love Street was rocking, and there was mayhem when the final whistle confirmed that, against the odds, Celtic were champions by the tightest of margins.

Hearts and Celtic had both finished on 50 points, but Celtic had the superior goal difference. Hearts fans have never forgiven St Mirren in general and me in particular for that afternoon, and some of the stories I have been told regarding my alleged involvement have been startling. On one Hearts website, you can read:

> One date is rarely far from our thoughts: 3 May 1986. Frank McGarvey, a former Celtic player in the St Mirren squad that day, was seen celebrating Celtic's title win at the end of the match with their fans. That left a very bad taste in the mouth, it has to be said, although, to be honest, no one really needed any extra excuses to hate Frank McGarvey! If there was no conspiracy, then McGarvey certainly did himself no favours.

I have heard that I was in the Celtic dressing-room afterwards drinking champagne, but that is garbage. I didn't see any of the Celtic players after the game. And I have actually met Hearts fans who have said to me, 'That must have been some party you were at the night Celtic won the league in 1986.' I wasn't at any party; I was in my house with my wife and kids.

I have also heard that the reason we lost so heavily was that the St Mirren team was packed with Celtic fans. Tony Fitzpatrick was a boyhood Celtic fan, like me, but that didn't come into it. There were also Rangers fans in the team, which, of course, included former Ibrox goalkeeper Jim Stewart.

Nothing can be levelled at me for that day. I hold my hands up to my reticence on my first return to Parkhead, but that was a one-off. I had played against Celtic another two times that season, and the fans hadn't sung my name. I had become just another former player, and in any case why would I want Davie Hay, the man who had sent me packing from Parkhead, to win the title on my new club's ground?

The simple fact is that Hearts bottled it. Nobody else was involved, and nobody else was to blame. Celtic were expected to beat us, and it would not have made any difference if Hearts had done their job. If Celtic or Rangers had had to beat Dundee to win the league, they would have done it, but Hearts did not have that winning mentality. I had just left Celtic, and the Hearts fans needed a scapegoat, but they should have looked closer to home.

I went to Love Street a few days after the end of the season, and there was a package with an Edinburgh postmark waiting for me. I didn't like the look of it, so I handed it to chairman Louis Kane to open. It was a shit.

13

....

SAINTS GO MARCHING IN
– THEN I GO MARCHING OUT

Our family holiday to Portugal in the summer of 1986 was **mercifully free of Hearts supporters and, as far as** Pauline was concerned, mercifully free of bookies' shops. When I was abroad, I wouldn't gamble, and it didn't bother me. I enjoyed spending time with my wife and kids, hanging around the pool or the beach away from the pressures of football. Maybe it was the change of environment and the sun that banished thoughts of horses from my mind, but once I returned to Scotland I felt under pressure again. It was a constant battle to keep away from the bookie's. I was still attending GA, but several months off gambling would be followed by several months on.

By the time the new season began, I was looking to get away from Love Street. Things weren't going well for Alex Miller, the team was struggling and, to be honest, I had begun to find the training boring. Years and years of the same exercises and drills had taken their toll. There was talk of me going back to Celtic, which came to nothing, and I soon buckled down to see the season out.

Alex left to go to Hibs just before the turn of the year, which I didn't think was a good idea given that he was an ex-Rangers player. Although he won a League Cup at Easter Road, I don't think the Hibs fans ever took to him, and he is certainly not revered in Leith for his achievement. I was sorry to see Alex leave but happy that I didn't have to chase full-backs any more. However, I was more concerned with yet another addition to the family.

Pauline was taken into hospital on the morning of 6 January 1987, the day of our game against Dundee United at Tannadice. I had missed Sean and Scott being born and was determined to be with Pauline this time. Alex Smith, who had replaced Alex Miller, said, 'OK, be with your wife and then get up to Tannadice as soon as you can.' I told the staff at the Rottenrow Hospital about my predicament, and they agreed to induce Pauline. Coincidentally, it was my mother-in-law Gladys's birthday, and she was at the hospital with me. I had a lot of time for Gladys. She seemed to understand my problems and supported me as much as she could, and I was thrilled that her first granddaughter, Jennifer, was born that day. I had never seen her so happy when I came out of the delivery room and told her the news. I made sure that Pauline and Jennifer were OK, and I rushed out so that my brother Andrew could take me to the hotel in Dundee where the players were having a pre-match meal. It was the strangest feeling, playing a Premier League game a few hours after watching your first daughter being born. I floated through the match high on adrenalin and pride. Although we were beaten 2–0, I played one of my best games for the club, and I was the only person on the St Mirren team bus with a smile on his face as we drove back to Paisley.

Alex Smith had been joined at Love Street by my old strike partner Jimmy Bone, who came in as his assistant – and they were inevitably dubbed 'Alias Smith and Bone' by the media. Alex was not one to take training; that was down to Jimmy. In fact, we didn't see a lot of Alex on a day-to-day basis. He was always in his office. After a while, we mischievously put a picture of him up on the notice board, hinting to him that we needed to be reminded of what he looked like.

By the time Smith and Bone arrived, we were out of the League Cup after a 5–1 thrashing by Forfar, and, as ever, we had no realistic chance of winning the league. The Scottish Cup was our only hope of winning any silverware, although a Hampden final seemed a long way off when we were drawn to play Inverness Caley and only 3,494 fans turned up at Love Street to see us ease through with goals by Kenny McDowall, Ian Ferguson and me. That was one of our good days, and on our good days we looked a more than decent team.

Paul Lambert and Norrie McWhirter, who came through the youth set-up, had good potential. Ian Ferguson came from Clyde, and he was Alex Miller's most enduring legacy. Fergie, like me and Paul Chalmers, was a match-winner, and he was eventually sold to Rangers for £850,000. He had a thunderous shot, and he scored one of the best goals I have ever seen, against Aberdeen, when he nearly took the net off with a long-distance drive.

We played rivals Morton away in the next round in February, and, in fact, that was the closest we came to being knocked out. We came from behind to win 3–2, Paul Chalmers getting a double and Fergie again scoring. Hearts had beaten Celtic 1–0, and with Rangers having been shocked by Hamilton Accies in the third round at Ibrox the field had opened up. All eight quarter-finalists had a genuine chance of winning the tournament.

After we had beaten Second Division Raith Rovers 2–0 in the quarter-finals at Starks Park thanks to goals by Paul Chalmers and Peter Godfrey, I genuinely thought our name was on the cup, even though we were paired to meet Hearts in the semi-final at Hampden. The Jambos were a good side, and I was well aware of how close they had come to winning the Premier League title the season before. But both sides had players missing for the semi-final. They had John Robertson, Brian Whittaker and Walter Kidd suspended and Neil Berry out injured, while we had Tony Fitzpatrick, Brian Gallagher, Peter Godfrey, Paul Chalmers and Gardner Speirs out through either injury or illness. However, the absence of John Robertson was crucial to our chances. Wee Robbo was a penalty-box predator almost without equal in Scotland at that time, and I had great respect for him.

In the semi-final match programme, I annoyed the Hearts fans further by saying, 'Hearts are favourites and rightly so. But for all that they are acclaimed as one of the best teams in Scotland, what have they won in the past decade? They have not won a major trophy to go along with the praise, and that must linger with them.' The thought of that parcel of shit had lingered with me.

We had the best of the first half and took the lead in the 33rd minute when young David Winnie, who had a great game as a replacement for Godfrey, set Fergie up with a magnificent pass and he waltzed around Hearts keeper Henry Smith and knocked the ball into the net. The tension grew as the second half slipped away, but we looked comfortable enough until the 74th minute when Gary Mackay grabbed the equaliser to knock the wind out of our sails. We rallied again, and a place in the final was up for grabs as the game drifted towards full-time. If there was one player the Hearts fans did not want to score a late winner against their side, it was me, but once again I had to disappoint them.

Alex Smith had told me to play wide on the left, and I had mostly stuck to my task, frustrating as it was. However, after Hearts levelled, I knew I had to take matters into my own hands. I moved into the centre along with Kenny McDowall, and I was confident that I would get a goal if only we could fashion a chance. An opportunity duly arrived with about eight minutes to go when Ian Cameron crossed into the middle of the penalty area and the ball broke to me off Kenny McDowall. I had my back to the goal, but I turned and volleyed past Smith from about ten yards out, and we were back in front.

The final few minutes were fraught, and you could feel the nervousness of the St Mirren fans sweeping down from terraces, but we held on for what was generally accepted to be a deserved victory. Once again, Hearts had choked at a vital stage of the season, but I could hardly have cared less as I celebrated with my teammates. To score the goal that put St Mirren into the Scottish Cup final was just as satisfying as scoring for Celtic in the final two seasons previously, and it earned me something of a backhanded compliment from midfielder Billy Abercromby.

Billy and I never really got on, although I wouldn't deny that he was a good player. I didn't like him from when I was at Love Street first time around, because I always felt that he sucked up to Fergie. As we sat in the Hampden dressing-room, with all the players still buzzing from our historic achievement, Billy turned to me and said, in a matter-of-fact sort of way, 'I don't really like you Frank, but I like you in my team.' I just smiled. It was to be St Mirren's first Hampden final in 25 years, and we would meet Dundee United, who had beaten rivals Dundee 3–2 in the other semi-final at Tynecastle.

I was also featured in the cup-final programme and couldn't resist having another dig at the Jambos:

I didn't regard Hearts as winners, and, indeed, my feelings haven't changed. They're a good professional side but lack that ingredient which would propel them to winners. I put United into that category, but only in Scottish Cup terms. They will never get a better chance to win it than they did in 1985. They were 1–0 ahead in the closing stages, and yet they still could not end their hoodoo.

United had the small matter of a European final to address at the same time as looking forward to meeting us at Hampden, and, as it turned out, they arrived in Glasgow 1–0 down to Gothenburg after the first leg of their UEFA Cup final in Sweden. We didn't take too much heart from that result. We hadn't won a game since beating Hearts in the semi-final. Two goals and two points in the last five league games wasn't great form, so we deserved the tag of underdogs.

I have heard the final described as the worst in modern times, and I probably agree with that assertion. It was a pretty boring game, but that didn't bother me, and I'm sure it didn't bother the St Mirren fans. It was the club's finest moment since they had won the trophy in 1959, and I feel privileged to have been involved. Our name was on the cup that season, and we rode our luck at times, but sometimes you need luck, and there have been plenty of times in my life that it has gone against me.

There was little between the sides in 90 minutes, but when extra time arrived I still felt confident. It was great to see one of the club's stalwarts and my good mate Tony Fitzpatrick, who had not been fully fit, come on to give the team and the fans a boost. The feeling that it was going to be our year intensified when United striker Iain Ferguson scored a perfectly good goal that was disallowed by referee Kenny Hope. A minute later, our Ian Ferguson grabbed the winner, forcing his way into the United box after taking a Brian Hamilton pass. The cameras don't show it, but if he had squared the ball to me, I would have had a tap-in; however, I quickly forgave him as he rattled the ball past Billy Thomson.

It was a fantastic feeling when the final whistle sounded yet so different from my 1985 cup win for Celtic. That had been about relief more than enjoyment. Relief at delivering for a club with massive and endless expectations. With St Mirren, winning the cup brought sheer, undiluted joy, and you could see that on the faces of the fans, the backroom staff, the directors and everyone else associated with the club that day. Most of them knew it could be a once-in-a-lifetime achievement, and they were going to enjoy it.

Many of the St Mirren players were winning their first medal, but I was as high as any of them. I was handed a ridiculous black-and-white top hat that appeared in all the pictures of the post-match celebrations. Paisley had not seen anything like it. We heard that one pub was selling beer at 1959 prices, which must have pleased the punters, but I think most people were euphoric enough. It was an amazing experience going round the town in our open-topped bus, something, of course, that neither of the Old Firm clubs can do.

After my experience following the 1985 Scottish Cup-final win, I shouldn't have been surprised when there was a little bit of sourness in the aftermath of the St Mirren cup victory. The club had given us a £1,500 bonus for winning the First Division in 1976–77, and we were offered the same ten years later for winning the Scottish Cup. I was raging, and as one of the senior players I went to complain about it. Eventually, after a bit of haggling, we got more. I was just annoyed that we had to ask for a proper reward for our achievement. After all, it wasn't as if they paid cup-winning bonuses out on a yearly basis.

On the Monday after our Scottish Cup win, we travelled to Singapore for a post-season jolly that incorporated a tournament called the Epsom Cup. We reached the final, but two days before the game I ate a local delicacy, based on eggs, which resulted in me getting a severe and debilitating dose of the runs. I was struggling badly, and in the dressing-room beforehand I told Alex Smith that I had nothing in me and wanted to come off in the second half. It was hot, humid and we were playing on a huge pitch. I didn't realise that he had used all his substitutes after an hour, and when I had nothing left to give I couldn't come off. The game was drawn, and they told us we had to go to extra time, by which time I could barely move. Someone asked me to take a penalty, but I was totally gone. I couldn't move. We won the penalty shoot-out, but I couldn't have given a damn. I was feeling so poorly that I just wanted to be taken to a hospital.

That incident really pissed me off, as did another a few days later when three of my teammates turned up for a team meeting drunk. Norrie McWhirter, just a teenager at the time, had loosened his tie because of the stifling heat, and Jimmy Bone told him to fix it – but said nothing to the three drunk players. Perhaps my disgruntlement was the origin of my later spat with Jimmy that caused such a rumpus at the club.

Most people thought that I was an instinctive, off-the-cuff type of player, and I do believe that the unexpected can make the difference in games, but I was a keen student of football tactics and how different managers liked to operate, so in the summer of 1987 I undertook my SFA A coaching licence at Largs. Andy Roxburgh and Craig Brown headed up the course, and I was delighted to be only one of three people, including my old Celtic teammate Roy Aitken and Tommy Craig, to pass with merit. However, it was Davie Moyes, another of my former Celtic teammates, who caught my eye. You can never tell who is going to be a successful coach, but I remember telling anyone who would listen that Davie knew what he was talking about. He never really made the grade as a player at Celtic and had a pretty average career, as I'm sure he would admit, but he impressed me with his thinking, and I have not been surprised to see him emerge as a top coach and manager.

The feel-good factor that accompanied our Scottish Cup success evaporated quickly at the beginning of the following season as we failed to win our first three league games and were then knocked out of the League Cup by St Johnstone. But our form had picked up by the time we met Norwegian side Tromsø in the first leg of the European Cup-Winners' Cup at Love Street. Kenny McDowall scored the only goal of the game, but the win was overshadowed by a dressing-room incident following my substitution in the second half.

I had been hooked along with Paul Lambert, and I was raging as I came off. I shouted at Jimmy Bone, 'What are you taking us off for?' and he said, 'Tactics.' I scoffed, 'Fucking tactics!' and carried on up to the dressing-room with Paul.

A few seconds later, Jimmy barged in. Before I knew it, we were having a rammy. I got a hold of him, but I was sliding around the floor on my steel studs, so I couldn't get a punch in at him. We wrestled for about a minute with Paul trying to stop us until he got thrown against the wall. Paul ran back out to the dugout, which emptied with the game still going on. The wrestling match was eventually stopped, and Jimmy was ushered outside.

I got showered and dressed, asked for some paper and an envelope from one of the office staff, wrote out a transfer request and had it in the boardroom waiting for the directors before the game had finished. Alex Smith called me the next day and asked me to come to Love Street. I had calmed down a bit, and I was hoping that he would get Jimmy in and sort it out. A handshake would have done me, because these things happen in football, but for some reason Alex seemed to want to prolong the situation, and he certainly succeeded in doing that.

I was unhappy with his stance, and I decided to withdraw my labour. I was playing golf the following Saturday when St Mirren beat Dundee United 2–0 at Love Street. I didn't return until 12 December, when I came on as substitute against Dunfermline and scored in a 4–1 win. The Tromsø game had been played on 16 September, so I was out for quite some time, and all because the situation wasn't dealt with properly at the time.

In the intervening period, we were knocked out of Europe. Although we got past Tromsø by drawing 0–0 in the return game, we lost 2–0 to Mechelen at home in the next round after scraping a goalless draw in Belgium. Mechelen continued on to win the tournament, but Alex Smith took a lot of stick for losing to a team most people hadn't heard of until that season.

During my time 'on strike', Alex had me in on my own in the afternoons training under wee Bobby McCulley, one of the club's coaches, and we would have a good laugh. Bobby was from Castlemilk, and he and his pal opened up a coaching school in the scheme called 'Castlemilk Coaches'. Not long after he advertised his new business venture, he got a phone call from someone wanting a 40-seater to go to the Lake District.

My absence created a bit of a stir, to say the least, and the newspapers loved it. At first, I said, 'I will never go back,' then it was, 'I might go back,' until I was so fed up I said, 'I will be back next week.' Throughout the whole saga, most St Mirren fans were on my side, and I was grateful for that. When I came on as substitute against Dunfermline, I got a massive cheer, which I'm sure didn't go down well with the management team.

However, a string of poor performances and results followed, and in April Alex Smith was sacked after we lost away to Dunfermline, who were relegated that season. He immediately blamed Tony Fitzpatrick and me for undermining him, which wasn't the biggest surprise in the world. Why was

I to blame? Even with my time away from Love Street during the season, I was voted St Mirren's Player of the Year. It was the players who had tried to keep Alex sweet who let him down, but he didn't want to admit that.

Tony was made caretaker manager, and I took up a player–assistant role. We lost 3–0 to Rangers in our first game, but a 1–0 win over Hearts the following week all but guaranteed our survival in the Premier League for another season. Tony got the manager's job, and I was made player–coach for the start of 1988–89 season. It wasn't a role that I enjoyed much. At first, I found it difficult to think about the team, how they were performing and what changes we should make, while I was playing at the same time. I started to think about pastures new after I had a fallout with chairman Louis Kane. He began to make life difficult for me, and at the end of the following season I accepted the opportunity to go to Queen of the South as player–manager. It was the biggest mistake of my football career.

14

··

PEEVED AT PALMERSTON

I had been happy enough working with Tony, but I wanted a fresh challenge and the chance to play more often. In my second season as assistant, I wasn't used much, and despite the difficulty of combining both jobs I still had an appetite for playing. Picking the team, of course, was one way to ensure selection. I took my first steps into management on my own on 6 July 1990 when I replaced Billy McLaren, who had moved to Hamilton Accies at the end of the previous season after Queens had been relegated.

I attended the interview with chairman Willie Harkness in the middle of the close-season, but they didn't give me the job until the week before the new campaign was due to start so that they could save a few weeks' wages. That should have been a warning sign, but I was blinkered. I wasn't going to let anything get in the way of my chance to be boss, including the advice I received from people in the game whom I respected.

I had asked my old boss Billy McNeill about the Queens job, and he told me not to go to Palmerston in a million years. I spoke to several others, and they said much the same thing.

But I had a career path carved out in my mind. I had been awarded my SFA coaching badge with merit, and, like all new coaches and managers, I wanted to see if my own ideas worked. It might have seemed as though I was taking a step backwards, but I thought I could slowly work my way up from the Second Division to the Premier League. There wasn't the same pressure in the lower leagues that there was in the top-flight. As far as I was concerned, the idea of learning your trade, as I had done as a joiner, also applied to football both in a playing and management capacity. It was and is an old-fashioned view, but it is one which I think is still valid. Too many players go straight from the dressing-room to the dugout in the top-flight, and it doesn't often work. My mentor Fergie blazed a trail from East Stirling to Manchester United, and if it was good enough for him, it was certainly good enough for me.

Things could hardly have gone any better for me at the start of my tenure, as we stormed through the early rounds of the League Cup. In the first game of the season, we beat Montrose after extra time, and a week later we welcomed Premier League side Dundee to Palmerston in the second round and beat them on penalties. I came up against my old Parkhead teammate Davie Moyes a week after that when we played Dunfermline, another Premier League side, in the next round at East End Park. I was playing at centre-forward and Davie was doing his stuff in the Pars' defence. Davie Irons scored for them with eight minutes to go after Jimmy McGuire had given us the lead in the twenty-third minute with a twenty-yard shot. Again, the game went into extra time, and again we came up trumps, Andy Thomson scoring after 102 minutes with a great header.

The most pleasing aspect of the match from my point of view was that we had been fitter than Dunfermline, which had made all the difference in extra time. I had brought the players in for extra work at the beginning of the season, and it had paid off. Even at the age of 34, I felt physically OK after the game, but the sweetness of the victory was spoiled a little by my former St Mirren teammate Iain Munro, who was Dunfermline manager. He refused to shake my hand at the end of the game, which wasn't the best bit of sportsmanship I had encountered. I suppose Iain was just disappointed, but the Pars fans were more gracious in defeat, and many of them stayed behind to applaud us off the pitch.

On the same day that we disposed of the Pars, the SFA sent out a letter to all football bosses warning them against fun bets for charity. Ally MacLeod, back as Ayr United manager, had been given a free £100 bet by Ladbrokes, and he had put it all on his side to win the First Division championship that season. If Ayr had succeeded, Seafield Children's Hospital would have benefited to the tune of £5,000. But an SFA official was quoted in the *Daily Record* as saying, 'Our rules are clear that no betting of any kind is permitted. We have phoned a warning to clubs but have followed it up with a letter, because betting on football is forbidden.'

It wasn't something that concerned me, as I was going through a gambling-free period. I was still faithfully attending GA meetings, things were good in my professional and family life, and it was the longest time I had spent away from the bookie's in years. Our League Cup run was giving me a buzz. After the Dunfermline game, I reminded the press that we were 'just three games away from Europe', even though I knew that we would be meeting Celtic in the quarter-final at Parkhead.

Before the game, I received my Tartan Special Manager of the Month award from Billy McNeill, which was a nice touch. We went into the fixture second bottom of the Second

Division, albeit after only two matches, but Celtic hadn't made a good start to their season, either, and had lost their previous two games without scoring a goal, so we felt confident we could spring a surprise. Billy had given me some of the best times I had had in the game, but I had no qualms about putting one over on him.

I picked myself to start, which didn't look like a good decision when Celtic defender Dariusz Dziekanowski scored after ten minutes. After surviving some near misses and missing some chances ourselves, Celtic seemed to ease up a bit, and we grabbed an equaliser through Thomson. I could understand how difficult it was for the Celtic players. No matter how much your manager tries to drum it into you that you have to treat every team with respect, you drop down a gear against sides who you should beat with ease. There is not so much adrenalin pumping, you leave runs and tackles that you would normally make to your teammates, who in turn leave them to you, and there is always the feeling in the back of your mind that if you do go behind you will be able to step up a level again.

The Celtic fans were raging at what they were watching. Billy had put out a strong team, but in order to shake the side up he had to bring on Joe Miller and Andy Walker for Martin Hayes and Charlie Nicholas, by that time back at the club after signing from Aberdeen. Our keeper Alan Davidson was in top form – he won the Man of the Match award – and I felt that another period of extra time was in the offing. But with seven minutes to go, Joe Miller produced a little bit of magic to score the winner from a tight angle, and that was our fifteen minutes of fame over.

It was the apex of my time at Queens, and things started to slide quite quickly after that. Coaching badges don't include advice on the myriad problems involved with being the manager of a part-time club, from block booking sports halls to dealing with players who can't make training because they have to work overtime or night shifts. Pre-season is all about getting fitness levels high, but it is difficult to maintain them during the season. It was frustrating trying to get all your players to turn up after a day's work, especially when we had no training ground of our own. And attempting to do any intensive work on set-pieces or tactics was almost impossible. We would train twice a week, one night in Glasgow and one night in Dumfries, but on some occasions we had nowhere booked, so the players were left to run around the track at Glasgow's Kelvin Hall.

The travelling was also starting to get me down, although I had a good club car, which I tested to the full on the M74. The difficult juggling act became even more difficult when Pauline fell out of a window and broke her back in a very serious accident, which ultimately kept her in hospital for six months. I looked after our four young kids during that time, stubbornly refusing help from family and friends. I was visiting Pauline in Greenock nearly every day, looking after the kids, and travelling back and forth to Palmerston. I was clocking up around 800 miles a week, and at times I didn't know if I was coming or going.

As if that wasn't enough, my relationship with Harkness had deteriorated, and it eventually came to a head when I tried to rid the club of several players who had begun to disrupt the dressing-room. Harkness had ruled Palmerston with a rod of iron for decades. His connection with the club dated back to 1937. He had been a Queens player and had eventually become chairman in 1967. He also undertook a long spell as SFA president and was awarded the CBE for his services to football, although I thought that he was the most self-serving person I had met in the game. Some of the other directors were more concerned with the social aspect of the game, and on long journeys to away matches they would occasionally take a cargo of drink with them and consume it at the front of the bus. One night before a game, I had to go downstairs at the hotel to ask those same directors to be quiet because the players were trying to sleep.

We more or less collapsed after the Celtic defeat. As the season unfolded, the players' fitness deteriorated, and our results weren't the best. I was determined to end the drinking culture that had taken hold at the club, and to that effect I wanted to get rid of at least four players. In my opinion, they were not behaving as professionals should, and they were also having a negative influence on the younger guys in the team. I approached Harkness to voice my concerns, thinking I would get his full support.

However, Harkness accused me of wanting them out just because they were 'his' players, which was too ridiculous for words. I couldn't have cared less who had brought them to the club; I just wanted rid of them before they did any further damage. The chairman and manager at any club have to sing from the same hymn sheet, but that was obviously not the case at Palmerston. Harkness was a sleekit man, and he reported back to the players I wanted out, which threatened to make my position untenable. It was all getting a bit much for me, and I thought about quitting before Christmas, but that was obviously not a good time of year to be out of work, so, against my better judgement, I carried on, struggling to keep a split dressing-room focused on football.

Therefore, I was delighted when Harkness wanted to meet me in a Dumfries hotel. I knew what was coming, and I was happy to oblige. I took Pauline with me, and we agreed to terminate my contract. Queens offered to pay me the £12,000 that they owed me, which meant that I was OK for the rest of the season. I had had good and bad times in football, but my six months or so at Queens were easily the worst.

It was a horrible experience, similar in some ways to another low point in my career that has niggled at me for years. I am absolutely certain that at least one game that I was involved in was fixed. Early in the match, the opposition went two up, and I knew even then that something was wrong. Our keeper fumbled a long-range shot to give their striker an easy chance and then he let in another long-range effort. He was a brilliant goalkeeper, so I couldn't understand what was going on. I couldn't do anything about it. I was helpless. Half my team clearly weren't trying.

I tore into them at the interval, but the culprits didn't give a fuck. I thought back to the time when I was told that St Johnstone would beat Queen of the South by two clear goals. One prominent figure in Scottish football said to me, 'Get all the money you've got and put it on St Johnstone to win by two clear goals.' I thought he was winding me up, so I didn't follow his advice. When I checked the next day, I discovered that they had won 4–1. It might simply have been a good tip, but there was more to it than that. My informant had been too certain. I didn't mention it to anyone else. Standing there in the dressing-room, I made a connection and thought, 'Is this game fixed?' It wouldn't have been the first time.

In April 2008, when one newspaper claimed that a player in England had accepted a £50,000 bribe to throw a game, it reopened a can of worms. In the 1960s, Sheffield Wednesday players David Layne, Peter Swann and Tony Kay were jailed for match fixing. In the 1970s, Leeds United manager Don Revie was accused by one newspaper of trying to bribe his way to the English First Division title in a crucial game against Wolves, and some of his players were subsequently implicated as well. An FA and police investigation found no evidence of wrongdoing. However, the rumours refused to go away, and shortly after Revie left the England job in 1977 the *Daily Mirror* alleged that a number of Leeds matches had been fixed during the 1960s and '70s. Again, nothing was proved.

In 1994, former Liverpool and Southampton goalkeeper Bruce Grobbelaar was accused by a newspaper of match fixing during his time at Liverpool to benefit an Asian betting syndicate. He was eventually charged with conspiracy to corrupt, along with the Wimbledon goalkeeper Hans Segers and Aston Villa striker John Fashanu. Although he and his co-defendants were cleared three years later, the stench from that case will never go away.

The problem hasn't been restricted to England. In 2004, there were newspaper reports that Morton players had bet on Airdrie to win the league after the Greenock side had allowed an 11-point lead over the Diamonds to slip. The rumours were so strong that two of the Morton players, Marco and John Maisano, sent out a press release via their agent Lou Sticca that read: 'In response to the rumours currently circulating Morton FC in regards to players of Morton FC allegedly throwing games, I take this opportunity to refute any involvement of John and Marco Maisano in such matters.' No charges were ever brought against them.

There is also a story that does the rounds in Scotland of one manager whose top scorer came off during a game at half-time, supposedly with a hamstring injury, and was then seen by senior teammates jumping around the dressing-room with his bookie's slip after his side had been beaten.

I believe that Scottish football is fundamentally honest, but there was definitely something wrong about the dodgy match I was involved in. Over the years, I have spoken to some players who played in that game, and they didn't want to talk about it. But I kept chipping away, and earlier this year one of the players who had given 100 per cent that night confirmed my suspicions that half the team weren't trying and assured me that other players agreed with my analysis of the game. The whole episode sickened me.

However, I could not afford to dwell on the past. I had to learn to cope with the sobering fact that at 34 I was out of football for the first time in my adult life. I had always been a confident, happy-go-lucky person, and, like most footballers, I didn't think that my career would ever end. It would be difficult to get back into the game quickly, so I had to consider a life outside of football. I knew that I was embarking on a new phase in my life. What I didn't know was that the journey would prove to be so traumatic.

15

....

THE FOOTBALL FINISHES

Driving down to the 'Buroo' in the Gorbals to sign on was a frightening and undignified experience. I had worked for 20 years and had no clue as to what the procedure was, what I was entitled to or how many times a month I had to attend. Also, under which trade would I be signing on? As a joiner or a footballer? Has anyone ever signed on as a footballer or football manager? The confusion all added to my depression as I sat in the waiting room ahead of my appointment. I was determined to make my DHSS experience as brief as possible, but I heard nothing from the world of football. I waited and waited, but the phone didn't ring.

Graeme Sinclair, my former Celtic teammate, advised me to buy a newsagent's in Seedhill Road in Paisley. Sinky had a newsagent's of his own, and he thought that it would be a good idea for me, but it wasn't something I enjoyed. I had to spend twelve hours a day behind the counter, from six in the morning until six at night, literally standing on the same spot.

I wasn't gambling at that time, but one day I picked up the *Racing Post* and noticed a horse that owed me a turn. I nipped out to the bookie's to back it, and it won. That was me back into gambling again, and, as ever, it escalated quickly. It got to the stage that I was closing the shop between 1.30 p.m. and 2.30 p.m. to go to the bookie's. Sometimes, I wouldn't get back until 3 p.m., and there would be people waiting outside the shop, which was quite embarrassing.

One weekend, I arranged to meet Pauline and the kids in Millport. She went down there on the Friday night and was waiting on me arriving with the money from the shop. But that afternoon I gambled almost all of it and didn't know how I was going to explain it to her. I nipped back into the bookie's with my last £20, backed a 20–1 outsider and luckily it won. I also won around £600 the next day in Millport, so we had a fantastic weekend. But I was depending on horses to determine which way my life was going. That was a hopeless situation to be in. And I had to sell the shop in the end. It wasn't making enough money.

Pauline was back to full fitness and taking care of the kids, so I found myself with a lot of time on my hands, which is not good for a compulsive gambler. I was back in the bookie's, and once again all my good work was undone. I began gambling even more than I had done in the past. I wasn't aware of it, but it was the start of a dramatic decline.

I found it hard to cope with being unemployed, especially when the Queen of the South money ran out. As the weeks went on, I was finding that I had nothing left after the mortgage and bills were paid. For years, football had provided me with easy money. Suddenly, being skint was being skint. There were no cup or league bonuses on the horizon, no sponsored cars, no interest-free loans and no friendly Scouse bank managers. I was an ordinary man in the street again.

I got a lifeline when, after being out of the game for a year, John Clark, by then at Clyde, asked me to help him out. It was coming up for Christmas in 1991, and I was glad of the signing-on fee to help me get presents, although the £20 per week in wages was little incentive.

Clyde had left their Shawfield home – leaving the greyhound racing behind them – and were lodging at Hamilton's Douglas Park when I joined. The side was floundering mid-table in the Second Division, and the supporters weren't happy that John had asked a 37 year old to help them out. I had lost all my fitness in the time I'd spent away from the game, and the first few weeks were extremely difficult. I was substituted in the first match, and in the following few games I could hear the fans audibly grumbling. When there are 60,000 people at Celtic Park, you only hear one big collective groan of disapproval when you make a mistake, but when there are only a few thousand the dismissive cry of 'Och, just come aff, McGarvey, yer hopeless' rings crystal clear. It was only a lifelong love of football that prevented me from packing it in.

John needed someone who was experienced to complement and guide the young guys in the side, who had plenty of running in them but lacked direction, and he was proved right in signing me. I slowly began to win the fans round. A double against Stranraer in January was a turning point. In the second half of the season, I scored six goals, but my overall contribution to the team was more important, and in the end the fans loved me.

But while I was enjoying playing football again – even if it was only a temporary respite from joining the real world – I was getting paid just £20 a week, so I was still skint more often than not. I started to get into more debt. I continued to ask my pals for money, and I was pestering my teammates at Clyde as well, getting loans that I couldn't pay back. People would ask me for their money, and I would tell lies to keep them at bay. As time went on, I lost more self-respect. I was embarrassed and ashamed about my predicament.

Only the football was keeping me going, and even that took a downturn when John Clark left the club. When Clyde director John McBeth told me that Alex Smith would be taking over, my gloom deepened. I told McBeth, 'I'm off. Alex Smith is not the best person in the world for me just now, and I don't want to play for him.' McBeth pleaded with me to stay, so I relented, but only because I liked the directors, players and fans at the club.

On 9 January 1993, after beating Queens Park and Brechin, we played Celtic in the third round of the Scottish Cup at Douglas Park. I was well into the twilight of my career, but I thought to myself, 'I'll show them I'm not past it,' and I did, setting up the chance that should have provided the shock of the tournament. The game was still goalless when I sent Jamie McCarron through on goal, but he lifted the ball over the bar when it was easier to score. The Clyde directors were probably as delighted as the Celtic fans. They knew that they would get half the money from the replay at Celtic Park. Our chance of a shock, of course, was gone, although we put up a decent display in our 1–0 defeat in the replay.

But there was to be one glorious finale. I wasn't the unhappiest player in Scotland when we won promotion at Palmerston in a 3–1 win. I was so determined to score down there that I pushed my teammate Stevie Clark off the ball when he was arguably in the better position. He wasn't happy about it, but I had to get that goal. Over the course of the season, I played 39 times and scored 16 goals. My Second Division medal meant that I had gathered the clean sweep in Scottish football: Premier League title, First Division title, Second Division title, Scottish Cup and League Cup. (There was no Third Division at that time.) It's something that I'm very proud of, and I don't think the feat will be repeated.

Yet again, a manager thanked me after winning him a piece of silverware by making it impossible for me to stay. I went to see Smith on the Thursday before the last game of the campaign against Brechin. I wanted to know what his plans were for the following season. I thought I deserved to be told, given that I was the club's top scorer and one of the main reasons we had been so successful. He told me that I had looked my age that season and that he would let me know within the next week if he was keeping me on. I felt deeply insulted.

On my way home that night, I made up my mind that I wasn't playing for Smith again. On the day of the Brechin game, we met for a pre-match meal in Bellshill, as was the norm. I asked to see him for a minute and informed him that I wouldn't be playing that day. He said that I was playing and would be in my usual position up front. I ignored him and let him know that not only was I not playing that day, I wouldn't be playing the following season either. With that, the conversation ended. I was still in my suit when we were presented with the Second Division trophy after the game. The fans were bemused, and I let the directors know my feelings before I left the stadium. The team John Clark had built up was dismantled. Next, Charlie Nicholas was brought in on £2,000 per week, 100 times what I was getting. Charlie didn't come close to scoring the number of goals that I had for Clyde, but his wages almost bankrupted the club.

However, I had more pressing concerns than Alex Smith or fanning the dying embers of my football career. I was on the brink of a crisis due to my gambling. Give me a 10–1 winner to start every day and I would still not leave the bookie's with money in my pocket, because I didn't know when to stop, which is, of course, the definition of a compulsive gambler. A win of £1,000 would not be enough to satisfy me. I was always looking for more. If I had won the earth, I would want the moon.

After leaving Clyde, I wanted one last payday from football, and a few clubs showed interest. Recognised goal scorers, no matter what age they are, are always in demand. John Clark stepped in again to offer me a contract at Shotts Bon Accord, the junior side that he had taken over after leaving Clyde. He offered me a £2,500 signing-on fee and £20 per week, and I of course accepted. Some of it went to Pauline, and the rest went on gambling. It was a stopgap, but it delayed my return to the real world a little longer.

When I was still playing, Jimmy Johnstone was driving a van for a building firm. I couldn't get my head around that, and neither could many others. The story goes – and it may well be apocryphal – that one day Jimmy said to one of his gaffers, 'What do you want me to do next?' and was met with the reply, 'If it was up to me, Jimmy, I'd put you up on my mantelpiece and leave you there all day,' a humorous indication of the esteem in which Jimmy was held by Celtic fans.

I identified more with Frank McAvennie, who, like me, had ended up at Celtic Park after leaving St Mirren. In recent years, he has played football with other ex-pros in Dubai, and I've read about how he has been doing this and that to try to keep himself busy and make money. He doesn't want to return to the real world and earn a living, but one day he will have to, and it will be difficult for him.

There are players who treat football simply as a job, but I never lost my love of the game, and I was happy enough to be getting my boots back on at Shotts. Others didn't share my enthusiasm. Lisbon Lion Stevie Chalmers said to me, 'What are you doing at Shotts, Frank?' The subtext was obvious: 'What are you doing playing for a junior side? You used to be a top striker for Celtic.' I was embarrassed, but I couldn't say anything, because I knew that he was 100 per cent right. However, I enjoyed my time at Shotts and got on well with my teammates. Dressing-rooms are the same the world over, no matter what level you play at. The Celtic dressing-room was the funniest I had been in, with some strong and witty characters, but in many ways the Shotts players were just like those who played for Celtic, Liverpool or St Mirren. They spoke about the same things, such as money, women, drinking, what was on television the night before and general football gossip. Professionals are obviously better players, they train harder, look after themselves more and play in front of bigger crowds – although some junior games get better crowds than lower league matches – but the dressing-room dynamic is constant.

The Old Firm dynamic is also constant. We got off our team bus at Larkhall Thistle's ground before a match just as two Rangers supporters buses were revving up to leave for Ibrox. As I walked up to the entrance, a Rangers fan spotted me. Word quickly spread, and all of a sudden the two buses were rocking as the supporters clambered up to the windows, snarling and shouting every name under the sun at me. It was a few moments of unrestrained madness as I watched 30 or 40 guys go ballistic. My Shotts teammates laughed, but I was just glad that the buses were leaving.

It all fell apart in my second year when the club was suspended from the Central Junior League for one season in 1995. We had to postpone a game because we had a lot of players out with illness, but the SJFA basically didn't believe us. The whole situation was a farce, but the upshot was that Shotts were disgracefully bombed out of the league. How could that be good for the game? I was glad that they were readmitted to the Second Division for the 1996–97 season, but the episode confirmed many people's perception of junior football as being a petty, self-serving and mean-spirited environment.

A few perceptions of my own were confirmed when I had a spell with Troon Juniors from Ayrshire a few weeks after turning out for Alan Rough's Glenafton. Roughie had no centre-forward for a Scottish Cup tie against Arniston and came down to St Mirren, where I was back helping the Under-18s, looking for a striker. I ended up being roped in, but it was never going to be long-term.

I was playing golf in Ayr one day when a guy who turned out to be the top man at Troon Juniors asked me to play for the club for one season. He offered me £1,500, so I agreed. I stuck the money in my back pocket without thinking what it would entail. I only lasted a few months. Apart from the travelling, which was a pain, I didn't like the locals. To put it in a nutshell, too many people were anti-Celtic. I was going to places such as Kilwinning Rangers and getting a load of abuse, so I packed it in.

This time, my football career was over for good. There were to be no more cameos or comebacks. My gambling career, however, was still in full swing and causing me loads more problems than a few drunken junior fans hurling abuse at me on a Saturday afternoon.

16

THE DARKEST HOUR
BEFORE THE DAWN

Pauline and I were struggling, albeit in different ways. I couldn't face up to being out of football, and she was not happy because there was no regular money coming into the house. She would look at my face when I came home and she would know if I had had a good day or not. I would give her a couple of hundred pounds one day then nothing for a few weeks. It was bad enough that Pauline wasn't getting enough money from me, but it was embarrassing for me and her when I started asking some of her friends for money – not for the house or the kids, but to get my next gambling fix.

I met a guy at GA, a manager with William Hill no less, who showed me a way to beat the bookies on greyhound races. I was desperate for money at that time and was prepared to risk almost anything. The scam relied on timing and gullibility. I provided the timing, and the bookies provided the gullibility. Big bookmaking firms don't like to pay their staff good money, so the behind-the-counter jobs usually attract older women or young girls, some of whom are part-time with minimal loyalty to their employers. If you picked the right shop, my GA friend told me, you could take advantage.

The scam, which seemed so easy, went as follows. I'd walk up to the counter seconds before a race started and hand over a 20p forecast. When writing out the betting slip, I'd bend the paper slightly to make it difficult to get through the machine that processes all of the bets. If my timing was good, the dog race I'd targeted would start at that exact moment I handed the girl my forecast. In my hand, I'd have another betting slip with the time and place of the same race, how much I wanted to bet (usually a much larger amount) and the word 'trap' already written on it, leaving me to quickly jot down the number of the dog beside it. I'd then look at the television sets behind her to see who was winning the race, and quickly and as deftly as possible add the trap number. Once a race has started, they shouldn't take your bet, but many of the girls are too busy trying to get your first betting slip straightened to be aware of what you are doing. I'd hand the second bet over, and they'd process it. It was then a case of hoping that the dog I'd picked wasn't overtaken in the latter part of the race. Sometimes that happened, but you'd be amazed at how many races are won by the dog who is leading after the first 40 yards. Of course, moving from bookie's to bookie's decreased the chances of the tellers picking up on what I was up to.

I tried it for the first time in a bookie's in Rutherglen. I started with a fiver and left with £100. I couldn't believe that I'd got away with it. I drove down to Ladbrokes in Bridgeton, and that was even easier. The woman was asking me if I wanted another bet on when the dogs were halfway around the track! I moved on to another shop in Glasgow city centre and again succeeded, and at the end of the day I had made £600 from a fiver. It had been embarrassingly easy.

I established a routine that gave me the best chance of avoiding suspicion. I would go to different bookies', limiting myself to a single race. With big winners, I would tip the girls and women behind the counter, and after that they would take any bet I gave them. I was in a bookie's in Bathgate and got a dog on at 14–1, an incredible price in a greyhound race, when it was ten lengths clear. I left with over £500.

There was the occasional hiccup. I got a friend involved in the scam, which was a mistake. We travelled to Renfrew one day to seek pastures new. It was a bookie's that we had never been in before, but there was a young girl behind the counter, so we felt confident. However, he picked the worst type of dog race to bet on. There were eight dogs running instead of the usual six, which decreased the chances of getting a clear winner. He should have waited until a six-dog race came on or left it altogether, but greed and impatience took over. He peeled off five tenners and made to put his bet on after he had staked a quid on trap one. A nightmare scenario ensued when three dogs came out neck and neck. He quickly jotted down trap three, which looked like it was edging it. He looked up and saw that trap five was ahead so scored '3' out and wrote down '5'. He looked up again and four had hit the front, so he scored out '5' and wrote '4'. Meanwhile, I stood watching this farce continue. The young girl looked at him as if he was deranged and shouted, 'Do you want another bet on or not?'

Trap two came through the field when the race was almost over, and my mate scored out '4' and had just enough space left to write '2'. I was nearly collapsing with laughter. The girl looked at the mess on his slip and refused to take the bet, barring him from the shop for good measure.

You could call it a scam, but as far I was concerned it was the bookies getting a taste of their own medicine. The bookies are no angels. Horse racing is notoriously bent. There have been a number of crooked jockeys and owners over the years, and if that is not enough to disadvantage the punters, the high-street bookies fix their odds daily to make sure they maximise their profits. There is nothing illegal in what they do, but most gamblers don't realise that they are being offered much lower odds than in the past. What was a 9–1 shot ten years ago is now priced at 7–1.

I continued for about a year and a half before they caught on. Then one day, out of the blue, I went into a bookie's, and the girl behind the counter said, 'I can't serve you.' Word had got round. Ladbrokes and William Hill both barred me from all of their premises, and the story ended up in all the newspapers. They need not have bothered; they would have got all their money back eventually.

I was sinking deeper and deeper into my gambling mire. The little flame that had been doused by the heavy workload at Queens was now out of control. I would not be stopped. There were other bookies and other places where I could indulge my habit. I spiralled out of control. I was in the bookie's from opening until closing, I'd then spend a few hours in the pub playing the fruit machines, and I'd then go to the dogs at Shawfield at night. I was a gambling junky searching for my next fix.

One of the more sensible things I did was sign the house over to Pauline. We had about £14,000 left on the mortgage, and I was frightened that I would borrow on the strength of it, in the form of a remortgage or a loan. At least I knew that no matter how bad things got for me, Pauline and the kids would always have the house.

I was in a daze and couldn't think rationally. My low point was when I took the last £20 out of Pauline's purse to put on a horse. She went to the shop for some groceries, and when she got to the checkout she couldn't pay for them. Needless to say, that didn't go down too well, and it was another nail in the coffin of our relationship. I was dragging her down with me. I was hardly an old man, but I wouldn't go back to work, which caused a lot of rows. I carried on gambling, hoping that things would sort themselves out.

When you have an addiction, be it drink, drugs or gambling, your mind becomes concentrated on your vice, and I became extremely clever at finding money. A bookie had once said to me, 'I've had a shop in the middle of town for 20 years, and I've never had a losing day.' That said it all, but he would have been as well talking to one of the racehorses that made him his money. I didn't care. I would lie in bed at night thinking of who I could go to for money the next day. My mind was like a computer. I would draw up a list of about ten people, then eliminate them by discounting those whom I knew were struggling or whom I had got cash from recently. I would then approach those on a shortlist of three or four and see how I fared. It was despicable behaviour, and I lost more than a few mates. Sometimes, I would be flush and bubbly, but too often I was broke and desperate. I was borrowing money from my friends, but I wouldn't give them it back, even though at times I could have £1,000 in my pocket if I'd won.

One day, I chapped on the door of my old friend Tom, who I hadn't seen for ages because I owed him £2,000. He thought that I was there to give him his money back and was delighted to see me, but his mood soon changed when I told him that I was struggling and needed more cash. He flew into a rage, shouting, 'You're a disgrace. You owe me £2,000, and you are at my door for more money?' But I knew he liked me, and five minutes later he handed me a grand and asked if I wanted more! I left his house, walked around the corner and jumped in the air as if I was celebrating a goal. Passers-by must have wondered if I was off my head. Tom's parting words, though, stuck in my head. 'It's not the money, Frank. It's that you don't get back to me or call. You mess with my mind.' And that's what I did. I messed with people's minds, and my wife was the biggest victim of all.

Pauline had been fully behind me for years, but even she came to the end of her tether. She was beginning to feel the pinch, and we managed to get by only because of her ability to cope with our increasing financial problems. I wasn't acting like a proper husband or dad. I loved my family, but my next gambling fix was more important than maintaining a happy marriage or spending time with my kids. Her parents had recently died, both at a relatively young age, and I think she must have said to herself, 'I'm not going to live for ever. I need to do something before it's too late.' I was not surprised when she told me that she wanted a divorce.

Pauline stopped speaking to me, and the relationship was over after she took the kids to her sister's house on Christmas Eve. I spent Christmas Day 1996 alone, and it was the most depressing day of my life.

We had shared a tragedy when our son Sean lost a part of his leg after being knocked down by the school bus. It was one of the most traumatic periods of my life. The bus had only caught the back of his ankle, but for some reason the blood wouldn't flow to his foot. He had to get two toes cut off at first as the doctors struggled to save his foot. I can still hear him crying, 'Dad, they've cut my two toes off, and they didn't even tell me.' I had to put a brave face on for him, but I was devastated. The doctor pulled me aside the next day and told me that if they didn't amputate below the knee within a day they would have to amputate above it. Sean was incredibly brave. He seemed to accept his fate, and his attitude was that he was better to get that part of his leg off and get on with his life. I was so proud of his stoicism. Sean was in hospital for about six weeks, and we visited all the time, but our son's plight didn't bring Pauline and me back together.

Eventually, the day I was most dreading arrived. I woke up on 15 September 1997 to news of my gambling habit and impending divorce plastered all over a newspaper. The banner headline 'GAMBLING SHAME OF SCOTS ACE FRANK' left little to the imagination. In the article, Pauline claimed that she suffered from stress-related illnesses, including asthma and ME, and also had a duodenal ulcer. But she had a history of poor health, so I was surprised that she was trying to blame me for it.

Her next step was to take out a court order stopping me from behaving in a threatening or disorderly manner in our home. One day, we had a blazing row. I wouldn't bite at first, but I snapped after she made a remark about my mother. My mother was in hospital with a heart problem, and Pauline called her an actress. To say something like that was despicable, and I lost my temper. When the police arrived, Pauline started crying and said that I had been shouting at her all day.

I was handcuffed and taken to the cells at the police station on Aikenhead Road, a couple of hundred yards from Hampden. The next morning, I was taken to court in a windowless van. I was handcuffed to another prisoner, who, as my luck would have it, was a Celtic fan. Worse than that, I was his hero, and he couldn't believe he was handcuffed to me. The feeling was mutual. He told all the other prisoners who I was and didn't stop talking until the van got to court. We were put into separate cells, the one I was allocated having another dozen or so guys already in it. I hadn't been arrested before, or been in a police station or court, and there I was, ticking off all three boxes. It was hard to take, and I sat there with my head down, trying to make sense of it all.

Another prisoner, whom I soon discovered was full of drugs, lay on the floor beside me. I was the first person he saw when he opened his eyes, and the whole place echoed as he bellowed, 'Franky Boy, what a goal in the cup final!' I was mortified as he began informing all and sundry about my career. 'Will this day ever end?' I wondered. Most of the other prisoners weren't really interested, but it was still embarrassing.

I was released after being charged with breaking the order, and I thought that would be the end of it. However, it seemed to me that Pauline wanted the charge to stick. I knew deep down that it was not her decision, but I was very angry that I had to go to court to prove my innocence.

Pauline took another court order out, this time banning me from the house. I rented a dingy flat in Victoria Road on the south side of Glasgow. The following months were a blur. The court case was hanging over me, and I was completely and utterly depressed.

The court date was humiliating and distressing. At one point, I saw Pauline sitting in a side room, and I felt sick. I had to come to terms with the realisation that my marriage was over. If I had beaten my wife up, I would have deserved to go to jail, but I hadn't.

Sense prevailed, and the charges were eventually dropped. I didn't feel pleased, just relieved. But the matter shouldn't have gone to court in the first place. I admit that the failure of our marriage was my fault, but having to go through a court case was extremely difficult.

In the divorce settlement, I agreed to give Pauline 80 per cent of the money from the sale of the house, but we wrangled over access to the kids. I didn't see Paul and Sean for about four or five years before we were eventually reconciled – but the youngest two, Scott and Jennifer, wanted to see me, which was very heartening. They had to sign a form to say that they consented to visit their dad, which was a joke. It typified the divorce procedures in this country, which are so heavily weighted against men. I empathise with the Fathers 4 Justice campaign, which has been growing in profile in recent years. No matter the circumstances, it is almost always the men who are made to suffer when a marriage fails and a family breaks up.

My suffering almost took me over the edge. Quite literally. A few weeks after the divorce was finalised, I found myself standing on the platform in Argyle Street Station. I was in so much pain. I had just lost my wife and four kids, and I was living in a dump of a rented flat with only a mattress for a bed. I was fighting a losing battle with gambling. I had no job, no money and no prospects. My life was going nowhere. I heard the train coming through the tunnel, and I thought, 'If I jump in front of this train, there will be no more pain.' I hesitated, then something made me walk back and hold onto a handrail. For a split second, I had contemplated taking my life. I knew I had to do something.

17

· ·

BACK ON THE TOOLS

As I came to terms with my divorce, I met a lovely woman called Jackie. I wasn't looking for a relationship at that time – in fact, it was the last thing on my mind – but it just happened. We got on really well and went out for quite a while. She helped me through an extremely difficult time. Slowly, I began to lift myself up.

Archie Stormonth and his wife Ann Marie continued to be supportive, as did Ann Marie's parents, Jimmy and Anne. They had some wonderful parties and the Burns' night when my long-term friends Bill Toy and Bill Shedden made us laugh all night long was particularly memorable.

Brian Murphy, a good pal of mine, offered me a job as a barman in a pub he had just acquired in the West End called The Arlington. I needed the money, but I was reluctant to accept. I thought it was a pub for old alcoholics, but that was not the case. It was a respectable establishment and one of the few pubs in

Glasgow where Celtic and Rangers fans mixed well to watch Old Firm games. Through the pub's regular golf outings, I became good friends with guys such as Ian Wilson and Kenny Lang.

I was with Jackie when I met Joe Boyce, a Celtic fan. I have met thousands of Celtic supporters over the years, but meeting Joe was a turning point in my life. I was 41 and had reluctantly accepted that my football career was over. During the course of our chat, Joe, a painter, said, 'Frank, I'm working on a building site in Drumchapel that needs joiners, so why don't you go back to your trade?' It took me a while to agree, and I tossed and turned in bed that night, more nervous than I had ever been before a big game.

I mustered as many tools as I could, and he picked me up the next morning. I felt as though I was being driven to the gallows rather than a building site. The gaffer was a Rangers fan, like most of the workers on the job, and he took me to see one of the houses. He told me he would give me £600 to finish one property, which entailed putting down the floors and putting up the partitions. I thought, 'Christ, it will take me a month to do all that.' I went back to the canteen to pick up my tools and get a cup of tea before I started. When I went back to the house that I had been in half an hour earlier, there on the floor, in splendid isolation, lay a big shite.

The steam was still coming off it, so I knew it was fresh. I thought, 'The dirty bastards.' Going back to my trade, back to a normal life, had been the hardest thing in the world for me to do. I didn't need this on my first day. I walked outside and thought, 'What am I going to do? Walk away or clear up the mess and get on with it?' It was 50–50. There were so many things going through my head. Was this the start? Would I be subjected to continual hassle? I swithered for five minutes then found a plastic bag, scooped the mess up with a shovel, bagged it and put it in the bin. I don't know what would have happened if I had walked away.

I needed someone to help me at first, but soon I was comfortably completing one house per week, and I stayed for two or three months. I was back in the real world, but it took another year or two before I got my confidence and personality back. I was up for all kinds of work, and Paul McNulty, the general manager of Mercado Carpets in Rutherglen and a friend, offered me a few shifts, which turned into a regular occurrence.

One day when I was in Mercado's warehouse, Alan Minster, owner of Alan's Furniture Warehouse, asked me to do some work for him at his store in Wallace Street in Glasgow. I went in a few days later to meet him and was introduced to his son Gerard and son-in-law Richard, two great guys. Over the following weeks, I did a few odd jobs for them, then I was asked if I knew how to fit laminate wooden floors. When I started my apprenticeship, most houses were carpeted throughout, and, in fact, having wooden floors in your house was a sign of poverty. However, fashions had changed: carpets were on their way out, and wooden floorboards were in.

I had never done one before, but I soon got the hang of things. It was another pivotal moment, if less dramatic than the incident at Argyle Street Station or my meeting with Joe Boyce. I thought, 'I'm inside, I can do the work and it pays good money – this will do for me.' I've been working for the Minster family ever since and have become good friends with Alan, Gerard and Richard.

Some people react in a strange way when an ex-footballer, especially one who has played for Celtic, knocks on their door. But my first taste of fame had been intoxicating. The day after I scored four goals against Reykjavik, I was sitting in the canteen at work. The guy across from me was reading a newspaper and sporadically staring at me. After a while, he said, 'I'm reading about a Frank McGarvey who scored four goals for St Mirren last night. Is that you?' I replied, 'Yes.' I felt ten feet tall for the rest of the day.

My profile increased further after I signed for Celtic. I was pounced upon everywhere I went: before and after training and games, when I was out and about in Glasgow, and at supporters' functions. The attention was fun at first, but the novelty soon wore off. Sitting at a table signing pieces of paper for hours on end was hard work, and after a while I realised that I didn't like being famous. I couldn't get any peace.

It didn't change much when I rejoined St Mirren. The players organised a fancy-dress party one night, and I was dressed up as a clown: wig, white make-up, rosy cheeks, the lot. I couldn't recognise myself in the mirror. Four of us got a taxi to Paisley town centre, and I thought, 'This is freedom for me. I can go out tonight and do what I want.' I stepped out of the taxi and a guy walked by and said, 'Awright, Frank? How are you getting on?'

The third phase of my fame – if that's what you want to call it – is how I will be for the rest of my life. I don't get pestered on a daily basis, but I do get recognised regularly, and it doesn't upset me. If signing an autograph or talking to someone for two minutes makes that person happy, then great. But to be honest, I would rather be just another face in the crowd. Tommy Burns articulated what all Old Firm players feel when he said that half of Glasgow hates you, and the other half thinks they own you.

I play a Glaswegian version of Russian roulette with a two-chamber gun and one bullet when I chap the door of a new customer. I look at some of the addresses on my worksheet and brace myself as I drive to my destination. I have worked in some houses where the people haven't spoken to me because of who I am. Sometimes I am glad that silence is all I have to suffer. I once turned up at a house in Bridgeton, where the husband, wife and some of their pals were having a drink in the living room. The picture of the guy on a white horse in the hall indicated where their allegiances lay.

The woman who answered the door was pleasant and polite but looked at me quizzically before saying, 'I know your face.' Before I had a chance to think, I replied, 'I used to live in Bridgeton.' She asked me whereabouts I had lived and who I knew, and I was getting flustered, so I said, 'I need to get on. I'm in a bit of a hurry.' I jammed the door of the room I was working in with a bit of wood to keep her out, but she tried to force the door open to get a better look at me. I could see her nose popping through the gap, and I said, 'Watch yourself, Mrs. I've got furniture at the door. It might fall if you're not careful.' I finished the flooring as fast as I could, then went downstairs to get paid. She settled the bill, then said, 'Who are you?' Because I had the money in my hand, I replied, 'I'm Frank McGarvey. I used to play for Celtic.' Her attitude changed, and the next thing I knew she was shouting through to the living room, 'Willie, Jimmy. Frank McGarvey is out here.' I quickly left before they had the chance to introduce themselves.

On another occasion, I was asked to go to a house in Merrylee to price a job. Resplendent on the walls were pictures of the Queen, Ibrox Stadium and that same wee guy on a white horse. Thankfully, the woman didn't recognise me, and I went about my business untroubled. I told her how much the flooring would cost, and she said, 'That's great. That's the best quote I've had. I think we'll just go with you.' However, her husband came through from the kitchen, recognised me and began shouting, 'What's that bastard doing in here?' She couldn't work out what the problem was and replied, 'What's wrong. He's very nice, and he's given us the best price.' Her pleas fell on deaf ears. 'I don't care. Get him out of here,' the man shouted. He then decided to take matters into his own hands. He literally chased me out of his house, and I again had to rely on a burst of pace to get away. On those days, I wish I was in any other city in Britain.

The flip side is that if I go into 'Celtic' houses, I'm treated like a king. The family all fuss over me. 'Sit down, Frank. There's a cup of tea. Do you want some dinner? We've got plenty left.'

John Cole, who helped me to get some work for Celtic TV, asked me to appear on a sports programme on Lanarkshire Television, which was basically a discussion about the forthcoming weekend's SPL games. It was a delayed transmission, but only by half an hour or so. I had a job to do in Holytown, just around the corner from the studio, so I finished the programme, had a cup of tea and turned up at the house still wearing the same clothes. I was invited into the lounge by the man of the house, where the rest of the family were watching me on television. They looked at me, looked at the television and looked at me again before it clicked. The woman started phoning everybody she knew – or so it seemed – to tell them that Frank McGarvey was in her house.

I would be lying, though, if I said I wasn't glad that I met the St Mirren fan who helped me buy a flat in Rutherglen with my share of the money from the sale of the family home following my divorce. It was a half down payment, half rent scheme, but I didn't have enough money to pay 50 per cent up front. The manager of the housing association, a Saints fan, told me that one house had been bought with a 75 per cent down payment, so he would be happy for me to buy mine with a 25 per cent down payment. He didn't need to do that. It was a lucky break for me, although, naturally, my luck soon ran out when I found a new way to lose money.

After moving into my new flat, I stopped gambling for a few months, and with the money I saved I bought a computer. I was close to being free from debt altogether – until I discovered Betfair, an online betting exchange and scourge of traditional bookmakers.

Online gambling sites allow you to bet against other punters when all sorts of sporting events, including horse races, are in progress. I had been banned from William Hill and Ladbrokes for my own version of in-race betting, but this was all above board. Companies such as Betfair simply act as a broker and take a percentage of the money gambled.

Bookies' are now open from 10 a.m. to 10 p.m., which is a massive increase from the days when I began gambling, but the online betting industry is a 24/7 operation. Traditional bookies will struggle in the future. They have to fix their odds to make sure they make a profit, which means punters lose out. Once people get used to betting online with companies such as Betfair, bookies will be under pressure.

To begin with, I was winning on the British tracks, but I then started to bet on American races, which I knew absolutely nothing about. That was my downfall. However, my dalliance with American horse racing started positively. I got up one night to go to the toilet and turned the computer on. I laid a bet on the favourite in an American race and went back to bed. When I got up in the morning, I had won £100. It was unbelievable.

I was bringing in regular money, so the bank gave me a loan for a car and a £1,000 overdraft. Before I knew it, I had used that £1,000 up. One night when I was trying to chase my losses, I asked for another £200 to be transferred to my account, thinking I had no chance. I was amazed when the transaction was authorised. Over the next few weeks, I ran up a bill of £6,000. My bank statement showed that almost all of it had gone on the betting exchange. The bank soon came calling. In desperation, I argued that because I hadn't signed up for such a large overdraft, I shouldn't have to pay it back, but they were having none of it. I had to get a bank loan to cover the debt. I was back in trouble. I had to remortgage my flat to pay back the loan. I was no angel in the situation, but in my opinion what they did was irresponsible and morally wrong.

My money problems escalated. The Inland Revenue took me to court and said that I owed them £10,000, but they had got their calculations wrong. After a lot of wrangling, it was agreed that I owed them only £2,000, but they still sequestrated me, which had a knock-on effect. My flat was sold in May 2007, and the profit from the sale, about £45,000, went to the sequestrator.

I was told that all my outstanding bills would be paid, but they weren't, which put me in a lot more trouble. In January 2008, one creditor called a newspaper and claimed, correctly, that I owed them money, and yet another negative Frank McGarvey story was published. The bills were eventually paid but the damage was done.

The divorce was bad for me, but, as is always the case, it was the children who were the biggest losers. I have been blessed with great kids, and they never ask me about the past, but they know that I never wanted to hurt any of them. As adults, they are obviously free to come in and out of my life as they like, and I always enjoy my time with them. Paul and I didn't speak for a while, but one night after we had a few too many drinks in the Glasgow restaurant Rogano he gave me a cuddle for the first time since he was a kid and told me that he loved me. It gave me a great lift. Paul is very hard-working, intelligent and has a good sense of humour. Sean has a degree in business law and has a great personality, and he has overcome his disability to play football to a high standard. Scott has a degree in computing and is doing very well, and he and his wife have made me a granddad twice over. Jennifer works for British Gas and is very clever young lady.

She is also an honest girl and didn't hold back from telling me what she thought of a draft of this book in a letter to me. She wrote:

I didn't think you did yourself justice, Dad. Although your gambling caused lots of heartache for Mum, my brothers and me, you have always been a fantastic father. I recognised your problem when Mum broke her back and you had to stop off after picking me up from school to 'finish a wee job'. You would then pop out to the car every half-hour with sweets. I remember thinking to myself, 'Will this job ever be finished?'

But you were always generous with your money, and as we got older my brothers and I would text each other when you had a win – we knew we would be guaranteed at last £50 if we saw you.

Some of my fondest childhood memories are of times with you, such as when you arranged for me to swim with dolphins in Miami when I thought you had forgotten it was my 16th birthday. I feel proud of how far you have come in dealing with your problems.

If only I could put into words what that letter meant to me.

My relationship with Pauline, though, is almost non-existent. We don't speak, but I see her every now and again at various family occasions – one of the kids' birthdays or a wedding – and we are courteous to each other. Maybe I should have some sort of relationship with her, but it would only bring back all the pain. Despite all that happened between us, I was glad for her when she told me she was getting married again a few years ago.

My relationship with Celtic fans is still good. Each year, two supporters from Ireland, Pat and Gerard Mulcahy, invite a few ex-Celtic players over to their pub, The Friar's Walk, a well-known establishment in Cork. We play golf and raise money for local charities, and we are treated like kings. In 2001, the Los Angeles Celtic Supporters Association invited my good friend Matt McGlone, editor of the Celtic fanzine

Not the View, over to the City of Angels, and he was asked to bring over a former Celtic player. Matt invited me, and I decided to bring my daughter Jennifer for a trip of a lifetime. She is extra special to me, so it was nice to give her a treat, and she absolutely adored Los Angeles. We also took a trip to Las Vegas – ironic, I know, but, amazingly, I didn't gamble that much.

I still follow Scottish football and go to the occasional Celtic match. Like all ex-pros, I have strong opinions on the game. I enjoyed my stint co-commentating for Celtic TV. The club at this time are in a very good position thanks to chief executive Peter Lawwell and the board who are guiding Celtic in the right direction. This is demonstrated by the club's third title win in a row for the first time since Jock Stein was manager and reaching the last 16 of the Champions League twice in a row. Celtic have achieved all this despite the financial constraints of playing in the Scottish Premier League.

A lot of Celtic fans expect me to toe the party line, and I get stick when I don't live up to those expectations. But I have to be honest when I am asked my opinion. I might not be the most diplomatic person at times, but I can live with that. Unlike most Celtic fans, I am a great admirer of Fergus McCann, whom I believe should occupy a bigger place in the hearts of the support. Indeed, I think a statue of Fergus should be erected outside the stadium. In the early 1990s, Celtic needed someone to guide them through the roughest period in their history. They had a stadium that was falling to pieces and Rangers were dominant. Fergus came to Parkhead, said what he was going to do for the club and did it. He made a few bob when he left, but so what? It was unbelievable that he was booed when he unfurled the SPL flag at the start of the 1998–99 season. Celtic fans are very knowledgeable about most aspects of the game, but they do sometimes get it wrong, and booing Fergus was wrong.

There will never be a statue of me outside Parkhead, but I did receive some appreciation for my efforts for the club when a guy called Jimmy Wilson got in touch and asked if I would mind if he arranged a benefit dinner for me. He had previously done something similar for Dixie Deans, so I agreed.

There wasn't a spare seat to be had on a wonderfully nostalgic night. It was great to see so many faces from the past. My old friend Tom Smith sidled up to me and said, 'I don't know what you've got, Frank, but you've got something.'

One of the auction prizes was a framed picture of me celebrating the winning goal against Dundee United in the 1985 Scottish Cup final. The bidding started vigorously and was soon up to £100, a bid placed by my daughter Jennifer. The auctioneer quickly shouted, 'Sold to Jennifer McGarvey for £100,' to make sure that she got the picture of her dad. After the dinner, Jennifer whispered into my ear, 'Dad, can you pay for that?' I ended up paying for my own picture.

I've moved into a lovely flat on the south side of Glasgow, and I'm getting on with life. My dad passed away in 2007, and that put a lot of things into perspective. Like everybody else, I'm not getting any younger. I've passed the half-century mark, and I just want to stay healthy and enjoy my kids and grandchildren. If writing this book helps one compulsive gambler, then it will have been worth it, but there is no traditional happy ending. I'm still struggling to stop gambling, but, if I'm honest, there are times when I am winning that I don't want to stop. The battle goes on. The flame still burns.

EPILOGUE

After Jimmy Johnstone's funeral in March 2006, the club organised a meal at Parkhead for Jimmy's family, friends and former Celtic players. I was sitting at a table along with Kenny Dalglish, Martin O'Neill and some Celtic players. Sir Alex Ferguson was sitting across from us, and after the meal he came over to our table, pointed to me and said, 'See that man there? I would just like you all to know that he was one of the best signings I ever made.' That wasn't bad.